2024 UK

Ninja Dual Zone Air Fryer Cookbook

Kattie P. Harrison

2000 Days Affordable and Healthy Ninja Air Fryer Recipes You Will Love to Save Your Time and Energy| with Expert Tips & Tricks for Beginners

Copyright© 2023 By Kattie P. Harrison
All Rights Reserved

This book is copyright protected. It is only for personal use.
You cannot amend, distribute, sell, use,
quote or paraphrase any part of the content within this book,
without the consent of the author or publisher.
Under no circumstances will any blame or
legal responsibility be held against the publisher,
or author, for any damages, reparation,
or monetary loss due to the information contained within this book,
either directly or indirectly.

Disclaimer Notice:

Please note the information contained within this
document is for educational and entertainment purposes only.
All effort has been executed to present accurate,
up to date, reliable, complete information.
No warranties of any kind are declared or implied.
Readers acknowledge that the author is not engaged
in the rendering of legal,
financial, medical or professional advice.
The content within this book has been derived from various sources.
Please consult a licensed professional before attempting any
techniques outlined in this book.
By reading this document,
the reader agrees that under no circumstances is the
author responsible for any losses,
direct or indirect,
that are incurred as a result of the use of the
information contained within this document, including,
but not limited to, errors, omissions, or inaccuracies.

Contents

Chapter 4 Dinner 25

Chapter 5 Vegetable and Vegetarian 37

Chapter 6 Sides and Appetisers 45

Chapter 7 Beans, Rice & Grains 51

Chapter 8 Fish and SeaFood 57

Introduction

Chapter 1: Air Fryer Basic Guide

What are Air fryers?

Air fryers? Do they fry air? Of course not! Air fryers are small kitchen appliances that cook food using hot air circulation. They are similar to convection ovens, but they have a smaller cooking chamber and a more powerful fan. This allows them to cook food more quickly and evenly and to achieve a crispier finish.

Using an air fryer is quite simple; just place the food in the basket and set the desired temperature and cooking time. Voila! Your food is cooking. The air fryer will then circulate hot air around the food, cooking it evenly.

Air fryers require very little oil to cook food. This makes them a healthier alternative to deep frying. They are versatile and can cook various foods, including french fries, chicken nuggets and tenders, fish and shrimp, vegetables, frozen foods, and desserts.

Still don't get it? Well, here's a briefly detailed breakdown of how the air fryer works:

- The air fryer heats the air inside the cooking chamber using a heating element.
- A fan circulates the hot air around the food, cooking it evenly from all sides.
- The hot air also helps to remove moisture from the food, resulting in a crispier finish.
- The perforated basket allows excess oil and grease to drip away, making air frying a healthier cooking method.

Why are air fryers so popular?

Air fryers are becoming increasingly popular and for a good reason. I would recommend them. But why? Well, they offer several advantages over traditional cooking methods, including:

- Healthier cooking: Air fryers use hot air to circulate food, cooking it evenly without
- needing a lot of oil. This means that air-fried foods are typically lower in calories and fat than deep-fried foods, improving your health!
- Versatility: Air fryers can cook various foods, from chicken nuggets and french fries to vegetables and seafood. They can also be used to reheat leftovers and cook frozen foods.
- Convenience: Air fryers are easy to use and clean. Place your food in the basket, set the timer and temperature, and let the air fryer do the rest.
- Safety: Air fryers are safer than deep fryers because there is no risk of hot oil spattering.
- Faster cooking time: Air fryers can cook food faster than traditional ovens, making them an excellent option for busy weeknights.
- Less mess: Air fryers are less messy than other cooking methods, such as deep frying or stovetop cooking.
- Energy efficiency: Air fryers use less energy than traditional ovens. This can save you money on your utility bills.

Overall, air fryers are a convenient and healthy way to cook various foods. If you are looking for a new kitchen appliance, I'd recommend an air fryer.

Chapter 2: All about Ninja Air Fryers

Ninja Air Fryers are the best in the market at the moment. They have garnered thousands of positive reviews and user feedback on selling platforms. Based on personal experience as well, they are worth the hype.

I have made a pick of their top 5 models you can consider. They include:

1. Ninja DZ201 and DZ401 models

At first glance, these two models appear nearly identical. However, a closer examination of their technical specifications reveals a significant difference that can help you choose the best suits your requirements. Ninja currently produces the finest dual-basket air fryers for several compelling reasons.

Ninja DZ201 Model

With over 15,000 Amazon reviews, the Ninja DZ201 emerges as a highly sought-after air fryer. If you're looking for a versatile and user-friendly kitchen appliance, this is definitely for you.

But why? It has an impressive 90% 5-star rating. This is a high degree of satisfaction among its users. A standout feature of the DZ201 is its Dual Zone Technology. This feature is also present in the DZ401 model. This innovative design incorporates two baskets, significantly expanding its cooking capacity.

What sets it apart further is the introduction of Smart Finish, a functionality that enables you to simultaneously prepare two different dishes, ensuring they complete their cooking cycles simultaneously.

Moreover, the Match Cook feature simplifies the process. I can now copy the settings of one basket to the other. How cool is that? This eliminates the need for manual input of temperature and time, which is handy if you've manually set these parameters instead of selecting a pre-set option.

Ninja DZ401 model

If you're in the market for the finest 10-quart air fryers, I'd recommend DZ401. While it is not as popular as the DZ201, it is a fantastic alternative, especially if you want a slightly larger option.

Thanks to its extensive temperature range, you can prepare various dishes and choose the precise setting to achieve your desired results. Its temperature range spans from 105 to 450 degrees Fahrenheit, just like the DZ201 model.

However, the DZ401 has IQ Boost, which differs from the DZ201. This feature ensures optimal power distribution across both baskets when you haven't selected Smart Finish or Match Cook. It proves invaluable for maintaining consistent results when simultaneously cooking two dishes requiring different heat levels.

Ninja Air Fryer Max XL (AF161)

The Ninja Air fryerAF161 is another excellent cooking appliance I'd recommend. Experience the benefits of healthier cooking with up to 75% less fat compared to traditional frying methods. Furthermore, up your cooking game with Max Crisp Technology, which delivers a searing 450 degrees of superheated air. This not only allows for cooking foods up to 30% faster than the Ninja AF100 but also results in hotter, crispier dishes.

Embrace the convenience of a spacious 5.5-quart ceramic-coated nonstick basket and crisper plate. This ample capacity accommodates up to 3 pounds of French fries or chicken wings. This is perfect for your family meals and gatherings.

Unleash your culinary creativity with seven cooking modes at your disposal. These include Max Crisp, Air Fry, Air Roast, Air Broil, Bake, Reheat, and Dehydrate. All these help you ensure you can prepare a wide range of delicious dishes. Say goodbye to the hassle of scrubbing and soaking, as it's effortless to clean.

Ninja Foodi Digital Air Fry Oven (FT102CO)

The Ninja Foodi Digital FT102CO is the ultimate kitchen appliance! Imagine a meal-making the power to air fry, air roast, air broil, bake, make bagels, toast, dehydrate, and keep your food warm.

Reclaim your countertop space by storing it neatly against your backsplash, taking up 50% less space. Enjoy healthier cooking with up to 75% less fat than traditional frying methods, as tested against deep-fried hand-cut French fries.

Its extra-large capacity offers 45% more cooking area than the Cuisinart toa-60 and toa-65 pans. It can accommodate a 13" pizza, up to 9 slices of toast, or six chicken breasts (6-8 oz. each). Cleaning is a breeze with a removable crumb tray and an easily accessible back panel for deep cleaning.

Experience fast cooking, up to 60% quicker than a standard oven with air roast, thanks to its 60-second preheat and the ability to prepare full meals in as little as 20 minutes. Its digital crisp control technology ensures precision-controlled temperature, heat source, and airflow for versatile and optimal cooking performance.

Ninja Air Fryer (AF101)

With Ninja Air Fryer (AF101), now savour guilt-free meals with up to a 75% reduction in fat compared to traditional frying methods. It also allows you to tweak your cooking settings as you desire.

Achieve gentle moisture removal or quick cooking and crisping with convection heat, ranging from 105° F to 400° F. The 4-quart ceramic-coated nonstick basket and crisper plate can accommodate up to 2 lbs of French fries. Family meals are no longer a problem!

It's equipped with four versatile cooking modes, including Air Fry, Roast, Reheat, and Dehydrate. Enjoy craft flat, chip-like dehydrated snacks with various dehydration options. The combination of low fan speed and low temperature ensures thorough dehydration. Furthermore, parts, including the basket and crisper plate, are dishwasher-safe. Simply wipe the machine's exterior to keep it clean.

Ninja Foodi 10-in-1 XL Pro Air Fry Oven (DT251)

Experience up to 10 times the convection power compared to a traditional full-size convection oven, ensuring faster, crispier, and juicier results. Cook better meals harnessing its ten modes, including Air Fry, Air Roast, Bake, Whole Roast, Broil, Toast, Bagel, Dehydrate, Reheat, and Pizza.

Achieve the perfect level of doneness, from rare to well done, with ease using the integrated Foodi Smart Thermometer. This saves you from guessing.

With a 90-second oven preheat time and up to 30% faster cooking than a traditional full-size convection oven, you can prepare meals quickly. Cook efficiently on two levels without the need for rotation. It can accommodate a 5-lb chicken and a sheet pan of vegetables, two 12-inch pizzas, or a 12-lb turkey. Prepare two sheet pan meals simultaneously for entertaining or weekly meal preparation.

Enjoy healthier air fryer options & crisp results; use the Air Fry function to enjoy meals with up to 75% less fat than traditional deep frying (tested against hand-cut, deep-fried French fries). Get up to 30% crispier outcomes compared to a conventional convection oven. The selected function illuminates the optimal oven rack positions, and the display settings remain locked when the door is open to prevent accidental changes during cooking. Experience up to 50% more consistent baking results than a leading countertop oven.

Why Choose the Ninja Dual Zone?

The Ninja Air Fryer is an excellent appliance, one I'd recommend you add to your Kitchen. It can definitely save you a lot of stress and make your cooking faster, better and healthier. Here are some reasons to choose the Ninja Dual Zone Air Fryer:

- Powerful Convection: The Ninja Dual Zone Air Fryer boasts true surround convection technology, providing up to 10 times the convection power compared to traditional full-size convection ovens. This means faster, crispier, and juicier results.

- Versatile Cooking: With up to 10 cooking modes in one appliance, you can air fry, roast, bake, whole roast, broil, toast, make bagels, dehydrate, reheat, and even cook pizza. It's a kitchen workhorse that can handle various cooking tasks.

- Precision Cooking: The integrated Foodi Smart Thermometer ensures perfect

- doneness at the touch of a button, eliminating guesswork and helping you achieve your desired level of cooking from rare to well done.

- Time-Saving: Dual zone air fryers offer quick family meals with a 90-second oven preheat time. It is up to 30% faster cooking than traditional full-size convection ovens. This is especially useful for busy households

- Extra-Large Capacity: The appliance provides 2-level cooking without the need for rotation. It can accommodate large meals, such as a 5-lb chicken with a sheet pan of vegetables, two 12-inch pizzas, or even a 12-lb turkey. Perfect for larger gatherings or meal prepping.
- Healthier Cooking: Enjoy healthier meals with the Air Fry function, which can reduce fat by up to 75% compared to traditional deep frying, tested against hand-cut, deep-fried French fries. Plus, it delivers up to 30% crispier results compared to a standard convection oven.
- User-Friendly: The digital display handle makes it easy to select functions, and the oven rack positions illuminate based on your choice. The settings remain secure when the door is open, preventing accidental changes.
- Effortless for Entertaining: You can prepare two sheet pan meals simultaneously. It's perfect for hosting gatherings or simplifying your weekly meal preparation.

How to Use the Ninja Air Fryer

Using a Ninja Air Fryer is relatively straightforward. Here's a basic guide:

- Read the Manual: Start by reading the user manual that comes with your Ninja Air Fryer. This will provide specific instructions and safety guidelines for your particular model.
- Preparation: Place the air fryer on a clean, flat, and heat-resistant surface. Ensure there's enough space around the air fryer for proper ventilation.
- Preheat the Air Fryer (if required): Some recipes may recommend preheating the air fryer. If so, set the desired temperature and let it preheat for a few minutes.
- Prepare Your Ingredients: Season or marinate your food as desired. Place your ingredients in a suitable container or air fryer basket/tray. Ensure they are in a single layer for even cooking.
- Select the Function: Choose the cooking function that best suits your dish. Ninja Air Fryers typically offer a variety of functions like Air Fry, Roast, Bake, etc. Use the control panel

to select the appropriate function.
- Set the Time and Temperature: Use the control panel to set the cooking time and temperature. Refer to your recipe or the air fryer's guidelines for the recommended settings.
- Start Cooking: Press the start button to begin the cooking process.
- Check and Shake (if needed): Depending on your recipe, you may need to pause the cooking process to shake or flip your food for even results. Some air fryers even have a reminder to do this.
- Monitor Progress: Keep an eye on your food as it cooks. You can usually observe the cooking progress through the air fryer's transparent door or lid.
- Finish and Serve: When the cooking time is complete, carefully open the air fryer. Be cautious, as it will be hot. Use oven mitts or a towel to remove the food and place it on a serving plate.
- Let it Cool: Allow the air fryer to cool down before cleaning it.
- Cleaning: After each use, clean the air fryer's removable parts like the basket, tray, and crumb tray. Many parts are dishwasher-safe for convenience. Read on for tips on how to clean your Ninja Air Fryer.
- Storage: Once cleaned and completely cooled, store the air fryer in a safe and dry location.

Remember to refer to your specific Ninja Air Fryer's manual for model-specific instructions and safety precautions. Furthermore, always follow the recommended cooking times and temperatures for your recipes to ensure the best results.

Tips and Tricks for Using the Ninja Air Fryer

Based on my experience with Ninja Air Fryer, I'd like to share some pro tips and tricks with you to give you a head start with the Ninja Air Fryer. They include:

- Use the Match Cook feature to cook different foods at different temperatures. This is an excellent feature for cooking a meal for everyone in your family, especially if they have different dietary restrictions.

- Use the Smart Finish feature to finish cooking two different foods at the same time. You can cook the main course and side dish together.
- If you're cooking multiple batches of food, preheat the air fryer between batches. This will help to ensure that all of your food cooks evenly.
- Don't overcrowd the air fryer baskets. Overcrowding might prevent the hot air from circulating freely and can result in uneven cooking.
- Shake or toss the food halfway through cooking. This will help to ensure that the food cooks evenly.
- Use a little bit of oil on your food. Slight oiling might be necessary to prevent the food from sticking to the air fryer baskets.
- Be careful when removing the food from the air fryer baskets. The baskets will be hot.
- Clean the air fryer baskets after each use. This will help to prevent the build-up of food and grease.
- Use parchment paper or a silicone baking mat in the air fryer baskets. This will help to prevent food from sticking and make cleanup easier.
- If you're cooking breaded foods, spray the breading with a little bit of oil before air frying for breading crispy.
- If you're cooking frozen foods, there is no need to thaw them before air frying. Simply place the frozen food in the air fryer basket and cook according to the package directions.
- To make your own air fryer croutons, cut bread into cubes and toss with some olive oil and seasonings. Air fry at 350 degrees Fahrenheit for 5-7 minutes or until the croutons are golden brown and crispy.
- To make your own air fryer popcorn, place a single layer of popcorn kernels in the air fryer basket. Air fry at 400 degrees Fahrenheit for 2-3 minutes, or until the popcorn is popped.

With a bit of practice, you'll be air-frying like a pro in no time!

Cleaning and Maintenance

Cleaning your Air Fryer is very important to ensure efficiency and longevity. I'd like to share my cleaning tips with you below:

- Unplug the air fryer and let it cool completely.
- Remove the air fryer basket and crisper tray. You can wash these parts by hand or in the dishwasher.
- Wipe the inside and outside of the air fryer with a damp cloth. Be careful not to get water into the electrical components of the air fryer.
- If there is any stubborn grease or food residue, you can use a mild dish soap and water solution to clean it. Be sure to rinse the air fryer thoroughly with clean water after cleaning.
- Dry the air fryer completely before using it again
- Clean the air fryer basket and crisper tray after each use. This will help to prevent the build-up of food and grease.
- If you're not using the air fryer basket or crisper tray, you can soak them in warm, soapy water for a few minutes before cleaning. This will help to loosen any stuck-on food.
- You can use a mild dish soap and water solution to clean the inside and outside of the air fryer. Be sure to rinse the air fryer thoroughly with clean water after cleaning.
- If there is any stubborn grease or food residue on the inside of the air fryer, you can use a baking soda paste to clean it.
- Make a paste with baking soda and water and apply it to the affected area. Let the paste sit for a few minutes before scrubbing it off with a damp cloth.
- To clean the heating element, use a soft brush to remove any food particles or grease. Be careful not to use any abrasive cleaners or scrubbers, as this could damage the
- heating element.
- With a bit of care and attention, your Ninja Air Fryer will stay clean and in good condition for many years to come.

Chapter 1 Breakfast

Banana Nut Bread

Prep Time: 15 minutes / Cook Time: 45 minutes
Servings: 8 / Mode: Bake

Ingredients:

- 250g all-purpose flour
- 5g baking soda
- 2.5g salt
- 115g unsalted butter, softened
- 200g granulated sugar
- 2 large eggs
- 3 ripe bananas, mashed (about 300g)
- 5ml vanilla extract
- 100g chopped walnuts

Preparation Instructions:

1. Preheat your air fryer to 350°F . Grease a 9x5-inch loaf pan.
2. In a mixing bowl, whisk together the flour, baking soda, and salt.
3. In a separate bowl, cream the softened butter and granulated sugar until light and fluffy.
4. Beat in the eggs, one at a time, then stir in the mashed bananas and vanilla extract.
5. Gradually add the dry ingredients to the banana mixture and mix until just combined.
6. Gently fold in the chopped walnuts.
7. Pour the batter into the greased loaf pan.
8. Bake in the air fryer using the Bake mode for approximately 60 minutes or until a toothpick inserted into the centre comes out clean.
9. Allow the banana nut bread to cool in the pan for about 10 minutes before transferring it to a wire rack to cool completely.
10. Once cooled, slice and enjoy!

Liver and Bacon Rolls

Prep Time: 20 minutes / Cook Time: 25 minutes
Servings: 4 / Mode: Max Crisp and Roast

Ingredients:

- 400g calf's liver, thinly sliced
- 8 slices bacon
- 1 small onion, finely chopped
- 2 cloves garlic, minced
- 15ml vegetable oil
- Salt and pepper to taste
- Fresh parsley for garnish

Preparation Instructions:

1. Lay out the slices of calf's liver on a clean surface.
2. Season each slice with salt and pepper.
3. In a skillet, heat the vegetable oil over medium-high heat. Add the chopped onion and minced garlic and sauté until softened and fragrant.
4. Remove the onions and garlic from the skillet and set them aside.
5. In the same skillet, cook the bacon using the Max Crisp mode until it's crispy. Remove the bacon and drain it on paper towels.
6. Wrap each slice of calf's liver with a slice of crispy bacon.
7. Secure the rolls with toothpicks.
8. Place the rolls back into the air fryer using the Roast mode and cook for about 5-7 minutes on each side or until the liver is cooked to your desired doneness.
9. Remove the toothpicks before serving.
10. Garnish with fresh parsley and serve hot for a sumptuous morning meal.

Breakfast Focaccia

Prep Time: 15 minutes / Cook Time: 10 minutes
Servings: 2 / Mode: Bake

Ingredients:

- 200g all-purpose flour
- 5g baking powder
- 2.5g salt
- 150ml lukewarm water
- 15ml olive oil
- 100g Greek yoghourt
- 150g cherry tomatoes, halved
- 100g feta cheese, crumbled
- 30g fresh basil leaves
- Salt and pepper to taste
- Olive oil for drizzling

Preparation Instructions:

1. In a mixing bowl, combine the flour, baking powder, and salt.
2. Add the lukewarm water, olive oil, and Greek yoghourt. Mix until a dough forms.
3. Knead the dough on a floured surface for about 5 minutes until it's smooth. Divide the dough into two portions and roll each into a thin flatbread.
4. Preheat your air fryer to 350°F .
5. Place one flatbread in the air fryer basket and cook

for 5-6 minutes, flipping halfway through, or until they puff up and have golden brown spots. Repeat with the second flatbread.
6. While the flatbreads are cooking, sauté the cherry tomatoes in a pan on the stove.
7. Spread the cooked tomatoes on the flatbreads, sprinkle with feta cheese, fresh basil, salt, and pepper.
8. Drizzle with a bit of olive oil if desired.
9. Serve warm for a great breakfast.

Breakfast Granola

Prep Time: 10 minutes / Cook Time: 15 minutes
Servings: 4 / Mode: Dehydrate

Ingredients:
- 200g rolled oats
- 100g mixed nuts (e.g., almonds, walnuts), chopped
- 50g dried cranberries
- 30g honey
- 15ml vegetable oil
- 5g ground cinnamon
- 5g vanilla extract
- Pinch of salt

Preparation Instructions:
1. In a mixing bowl, combine the rolled oats, mixed nuts, and dried cranberries.
2. In a separate bowl, whisk together the honey, vegetable oil, ground cinnamon, vanilla extract, and a pinch of salt.
3. Pour the honey mixture over the oat mixture and stir until everything is well coated.
4. Preheat your air fryer to the Dehydrate mode.
5. Spread the granola mixture evenly in the air fryer basket.
6. Dehydrate the granola for about 15 minutes or until it reaches your desired level of crispiness, stirring occasionally.
7. Allow the granola to cool completely before storing it in an airtight container.
8. Serve with yoghourt, milk, or as a topping for your favourite breakfast dishes. Enjoy!

Breakfast Breads with Clotted Cream and Jam

Prep Time: 15 minutes / Cook Time: 10 minutes
Servings: 2 / Mode: Bake

Ingredients:
- 200g assorted breakfast bread rolls (e.g.,

croissants, brioche)
- 100g clotted cream
- 100g fruit jam (e.g., strawberry, raspberry)
- Fresh berries for garnish (optional)

Preparation Instructions:
1. Preheat your air fryer to 350°F .
2. Place the assorted breakfast bread rolls in the air fryer basket.
3. Using the Bake mode, cook the bread rolls for about 5-7 minutes until they become warm and slightly toasted.
4. While the bread rolls are warming, prepare small bowls with clotted cream and fruit jam for dipping.
5. Once the bread rolls are ready, remove them from the air fryer.
6. Serve the warm bread rolls with clotted cream, jam, and fresh berries if desired.

Scottish Crowdie Cheese with Oatcakes

Prep Time: 10 minutes / Cook Time: 5 minutes
Servings: 4 / Mode: Air Fry

Ingredients:
- 200g Scottish Crowdie cheese
- 100g oatcakes
- 50g honey
- Fresh thyme leaves for garnish (optional)

Preparation Instructions:
1. Slice the Scottish Crowdie cheese into small portions for serving.
2. Arrange the oatcakes on a serving platter.
3. Preheat your air fryer to the Air Fry mode.
4. Place the oatcakes in the air fryer basket.
5. Air fry the oatcakes at a low temperature (around 300°F) for about 5 minutes, checking them frequently to ensure they become crispy.
6. Once the oatcakes are adequately crispy, remove them from the air fryer.
7. Arrange the Scottish Crowdie cheese slices on the oatcakes.
8. Drizzle honey over the cheese and oatcakes.
9. Garnish with fresh thyme leaves if desired.

Apple Turnovers

Prep Time: 20 minutes / Cook Time: 15 minutes
Servings: 4 / Mode: Bake

Ingredients:
- 2 sheets of puff pastry, thawed
- 2 medium apples, peeled, cored, and diced

- 50g granulated sugar
- 5g ground cinnamon
- 15g unsalted butter
- 1 egg, beaten (for egg wash)
- Powdered sugar for dusting (optional)

Preparation Instructions:

1. In a skillet, melt the unsalted butter over medium heat. Add the diced apples, granulated sugar, and ground cinnamon. Sauté until the apples are tender and caramelised. Remove from heat and let it cool.
2. Preheat your air fryer to 375°F.
3. Roll out the puff pastry sheets and cut each into four squares.
4. Place a spoonful of the caramelised apple mixture onto the centre of each puff pastry square.
5. Fold each square in half diagonally, forming a triangle. Press the edges to seal.
6. Brush the tops of the turnovers with beaten egg to give them a golden finish.
7. Place the turnovers in the air fryer basket.
8. Using the Bake mode, cook the turnovers for about 10-12 minutes, or until they are puffed and golden brown.
9. Remove the turnovers from the air fryer and let them cool slightly.

Cinnamon Sugar Pretzel

Prep Time: 15 minutes / Cook Time: 10 minutes
Servings: 4 / Mode: Air Fry

Ingredients:

- 200g pizza dough (store-bought or homemade)
- 30g unsalted butter, melted
- 50g granulated sugar
- 5g ground cinnamon

Preparation Instructions:

1. Preheat your air fryer to 350°F .
2. Roll out the pizza dough into a rectangle on a lightly floured surface.
3. Cut the dough into thin strips, like long pretzel sticks.
4. In a bowl, mix together the granulated sugar and ground cinnamon.
5. Dip each dough strip into the melted butter, then roll it in the cinnamon sugar mixture to coat.
6. Place the coated dough strips in the air fryer basket.
7. Air fry the cinnamon sugar pretzels using the Air Fry mode for about 6-8 minutes, or until they become golden brown and crispy.
8. Remove the pretzels from the air fryer and let them cool slightly before serving.

Dutch Baby Pancakes

Prep Time: 10 minutes / Cook Time: 15 minutes
Servings: 2 / Mode: Bake

Ingredients:

- 2 large eggs
- 60g all-purpose flour
- 75ml milk
- 5g granulated sugar
- 2.5g vanilla extract
- Pinch of salt
- 15g unsalted butter
- Powdered sugar and fresh berries for garnish (optional)

Preparation Instructions:

1. Preheat your air fryer to 400°F.
2. In a blender, combine the eggs, flour, milk, granulated sugar, vanilla extract, and a pinch of salt. Blend until the batter is smooth.
3. Place the unsalted butter in an oven-safe skillet or dish and put it in the preheated air fryer for about 1 minute or until the butter melts and begins to sizzle.
4. Pour the batter into the skillet with the melted butter.
5. Using the Bake mode, cook the Dutch Baby Pancake for about 12-15 minutes or until it puffs up and turns golden brown.
6. Remove the skillet from the air fryer.
7. Optionally, garnish with powdered sugar and fresh berries.
8. Slice and serve your Dutch Baby Pancake immediately for the best enjoyment.

Waffles with Berries

Prep Time: 10 minutes / Cook Time: 10 minutes
Servings: 4 / Mode: Bake

Ingredients:

- 200g all-purpose flour
- 5g baking powder
- 2.5g salt
- 30g granulated sugar
- 2 large eggs
- 240ml milk
- 60ml vegetable oil
- Fresh berries (e.g., strawberries, blueberries, raspberries) for topping

Preparation Instructions:

1. Preheat your air fryer to 360°F.
2. In a mixing bowl, whisk together the flour, baking

powder, salt, and granulated sugar.

3. In a separate bowl, beat the eggs and then add the milk and vegetable oil. Mix well.
4. Pour the wet ingredients into the dry ingredients and stir until the batter is smooth.
5. Lightly grease the waffle plates of your air fryer.
6. Pour the waffle batter onto the plates, spreading it evenly.
7. Close the air fryer and cook the waffles using the Bake mode for about 6-8 minutes or until they are golden brown and crisp.
8. Carefully remove the waffles from the air fryer.
9. Top your waffles with fresh berries and a drizzle of syrup if desired.
10. Serve your delicious Waffles with Berries for a delightful breakfast or brunch.

Sausage and Egg Biscuits

Prep Time: 15 minutes / Cook Time: 10 minutes
Servings: 4 / Mode: Bake

Ingredients:
- 4 biscuits (store-bought or homemade)
- 4 cooked breakfast sausage patties
- 4 large eggs
- Salt and pepper to taste
- Slices of cheese (optional)
- Butter for greasing

Preparation Instructions:
1. Preheat your air fryer to 350°F .
2. Split the biscuits in half and place them on a baking sheet.
3. Place one cooked breakfast sausage patty on the bottom half of each biscuit.
4. Crack one egg onto each sausage patty. Season with salt and pepper.
5. Optionally, add a slice of cheese on top of the eggs.
6. Place the top halves of the biscuits over the eggs to form sandwiches.
7. Grease the air fryer basket with a little butter.
8. Using the Bake mode, cook the sandwiches for about 8-10 minutes or until the biscuits are golden brown, the eggs are cooked to your desired level, and the cheese is melted (if used).
9. Remove the Sausage and Egg Biscuits from the air fryer.
10. Serve your delicious breakfast sandwiches hot.

Sugar French Toast Sticks

Prep Time: 10 minutes / Cook Time: 10 minutes
Servings: 4 / Mode: Air Fry

Ingredients:
- 8 slices of bread, cut into strips
- 2 large eggs
- 60ml milk
- 30g granulated sugar
- 5g ground cinnamon
- Powdered sugar for dusting (optional)
- Maple syrup for dipping

Preparation Instructions:
1. In a mixing bowl, whisk together the eggs, milk, granulated sugar, and ground cinnamon.
2. Dip the bread strips into the egg mixture ensuring they are well coated.
3. Preheat your air fryer to 350°F .
4. Place the coated bread strips in the air fryer basket, making sure they are not overcrowded.
5. Air fry the French toast sticks using the Air Fry mode for about 4-5 minutes on each side, or until they become golden brown and crispy.
6. Remove the French toast sticks from the air fryer.
7. Optionally, dust with powdered sugar before serving.

Sausage and Black Pudding Baps

Prep Time: 15 minutes / Cook Time: 10 minutes
Servings: 4 / Mode: Bake

Ingredients:
- 4 baps or soft rolls
- 8 cooked pork sausages
- 200g black pudding, sliced
- Ketchup or brown sauce (optional)
- Butter for greasing

Preparation Instructions:
1. Preheat your air fryer to 350°F .
2. Slice the baps in half and spread them open
3. Place 2 cooked pork sausages and a portion of sliced black pudding inside each bap.
4. Optionally, add ketchup or brown sauce for extra flavor.
5. Grease the air fryer basket with a little butter.
6. Using the Bake mode, cook the Sausage and Black Pudding Baps for about 8-10 minutes or until the baps are lightly toasted, and the sausages and black pudding are heated through.
7. Remove the baps from the air fryer.
8. Serve your delicious Sausage and Black Pudding Baps hot.

Chocolate Lava Cakes

Prep Time: 15 minutes / Cook Time: 10 minutes
Servings: 4 / Mode: Bake

Ingredients:

- 100g dark chocolate
- 60g unsalted butter
- 2 large eggs
- 50g granulated sugar
- 30g all-purpose flour
- 5ml vanilla extract
- Cocoa powder for dusting (optional)
- Vanilla ice cream (optional)

Preparation Instructions:

1. Preheat your air fryer to 375°F.
2. In a microwave-safe bowl, melt the dark chocolate and unsalted butter together in the microwave, stirring until smooth. Let it cool slightly.
3. In a separate bowl, whisk together the eggs and granulated sugar until well combined.
4. Pour the melted chocolate mixture into the egg mixture and stir well.
5. Add the all-purpose flour and vanilla extract, and mix until you have a smooth batter.
6. Grease four ramekins or oven-safe dishes with a little butter.
7. Divide the chocolate batter equally among the ramekins.
8. Using the Bake mode, cook the Chocolate Lava Cakes in the air fryer for about 8-10 minutes or until the cakes have set around the edges but are still soft in the centre.
9. Remove the lava cakes from the air fryer and serve hot.

Breakfast Crepes with Nutella

Prep Time: 15 minutes / Cook Time: 10 minutes
Servings: 4 / Mode: Bake

Ingredients:

- 125g all-purpose flour
- 2 large eggs
- 240ml milk
- 15ml vegetable oil
- Pinch of salt
- Nutella or chocolate hazelnut spread
- Sliced bananas, strawberries, or berries for filling (optional)
- Powdered sugar for dusting (optional)

Preparation Instructions:

1. In a blender, combine the all-purpose flour, eggs, milk, vegetable oil, and a pinch of salt. Blend until the crepe batter is smooth.
2. Preheat your air fryer to 375°F.
3. Lightly grease the air fryer basket with oil.
4. Pour a small amount of crepe batter into the centre of the air fryer basket, swirling it around to create a thin, even layer.
5. Using the Bake mode, cook the crepe for about 2-3 minutes or until it becomes lightly golden. Repeat this step for each crepe.
6. Carefully remove each crepe from the air fryer and spread Nutella or chocolate hazelnut spread over one half.
7. Add sliced bananas, strawberries, or berries if desired.
8. Fold the crepe in half to create a semi-circle.
9. Optionally, dust with powdered sugar.

Breakfast Dutch Baby

Prep Time: 10 minutes / Cook Time: 15 minutes
Servings: 2 / Mode: Bake

Ingredients:

- 2 large eggs
- 60g all-purpose flour
- 120ml milk
- 5g granulated sugar
- 2.5g vanilla extract
- Pinch of salt
- 15g unsalted butter
- Powdered sugar for dusting (optional)
- Fresh berries or fruit for topping (optional)

Preparation Instructions:

1. Preheat your air fryer to 400°F.
2. In a blender, combine the eggs, all-purpose flour, milk, granulated sugar, vanilla extract, and a pinch of salt. Blend until the Dutch Baby batter is smooth.
3. Place the unsalted butter in an oven-safe skillet or dish and put it in the preheated air fryer for about 1 minute or until the butter melts and starts to sizzle.
4. Pour the Dutch Baby batter into the skillet with the melted butter.
5. Using the Bake mode, cook the Dutch Baby for about 12-15 minutes or until it puffs up and turns golden brown.
6. Remove the Dutch Baby from the air fryer.
7. Optionally, dust with powdered sugar and top with fresh berries or fruit.

Breakfast Popovers

Prep Time: 10 minutes / Cook Time: 20 minutes
Servings: 6 / Mode: Bake

Ingredients:

- 2 large eggs
- 240ml milk
- 120g all-purpose flour
- Pinch of salt
- 15g unsalted butter, melted
- 30g shredded cheddar cheese (optional)
- 30g cooked bacon bits (optional)
- Fresh herbs (e.g., chives, parsley) for garnish (optional)

Preparation Instructions:

1. Preheat your air fryer to 375°F.
2. In a mixing bowl, whisk together the eggs and milk until well combined.
3. Gradually add the all-purpose flour and a pinch of salt, whisking until the batter is smooth.
4. Stir in the melted butter and mix until incorporated.
5. Optionally, add shredded cheddar cheese and cooked bacon bits to the batter for extra flavor.
6. Grease the cups of a popover pan or muffin tin with a little butter or cooking spray.
7. Fill each cup halfway with the popover batter.
8. Place the popover pan in the preheated air fryer using the Bake mode.
9. Cook the popovers for about 15-20 minutes or until they are puffed and golden brown.
10. Optionally, garnish with fresh herbs before serving.
11. Serve your Breakfast Popovers hot.

Breakfast Eclairs

Prep Time: 20 minutes / Cook Time: 20 minutes
Servings: 4 / Mode: Bake

Ingredients:

- For the Éclair Pastry:
- 60g unsalted butter
- 120ml water
- 75g all-purpose flour
- 2 large eggs
- For the Filling and Topping:
- 120g whipped cream
- 30g chocolate chips
- 15g powdered sugar for dusting

Preparation Instructions:
For the Éclair Pastry:

1. Preheat your air fryer to 375°F.
2. In a saucepan, combine the unsalted butter and water. Heat over medium heat until the butter is melted and the mixture begins to boil.
3. Remove from heat and quickly stir in the all-purpose flour until the mixture forms a smooth dough.
4. Let the dough cool slightly.
5. Beat in the eggs, one at a time, until the dough is smooth and glossy.
6. Transfer the dough to a piping bag or a plastic storage bag with a corner snipped off.
7. Pipe the dough into éclair shapes on a greased air fryer basket or tray.
8. Using the Bake mode, cook the éclairs for about 15-20 minutes or until they are golden brown and hollow inside.

For the Filling and Topping:

9. Allow the éclairs to cool completely.
10. Whip the cream until it holds stiff peaks.
11. Melt the chocolate chips in a microwave or on a stovetop.
12. Slice the cooled éclairs in half horizontally.
13. Fill each éclair with whipped cream and drizzle with melted chocolate.
14. Dust with powdered sugar for an elegant finish.
15. Serve your Breakfast Éclairs as a delightful breakfast and enjoy.

Breakfast Tamales

Prep Time: 30 minutes / Cook Time: 20 minutes
Servings: 4 / Mode: Air Fry

Ingredients:

- For the Tamale Filling:
- 240g Shredded chicken
- 240ml Salsa
- 60g Diced green bell pepper
- 60g Diced onion
- 60g Shredded cheddar cheese
- 3g Salt
- 2g Pepper
- For the Tamale Dough:
- 120g Masa harina (corn flour)
- 240ml Chicken broth
- 30ml Vegetable oil
- 2.5g Baking powder
- Pinch of salt

Preparation Instructions:

- For the Tamale Filling:
1. Combine 240g shredded chicken, 240ml salsa, 60g diced green bell pepper, 60g diced onion, 60g

shredded cheddar cheese, 3g salt, and 2g pepper. Mix well.

For the Tamale Dough:

2. In a separate bowl, combine 120g masa harina (corn flour), 240ml chicken broth, 30ml vegetable oil, 2.5g baking powder, and a pinch of salt. Mix until a soft dough forms.
3. Take a small portion of the tamale dough and press it flat in the palm of your hand.
4. Place a spoonful of the tamale filling in the centre of the dough.
5. Fold the dough around the filling to form a tamale shape. Repeat this step for all the tamales.

Breakfast Naan

Prep Time: 10 minutes / Cook Time: 10 minutes
Servings: 4 / Mode: Bake

Ingredients:

- Naan bread
- Eggs
- Spinach leaves
- Diced tomatoes
- Crumbled feta cheese
- Olive oil for brushing
- Salt and pepper to taste

Preparation `Instructions:

1. Preheat your air fryer to 375°F.
2. Brush each piece of naan bread with a little olive oil.
3. Place the naan bread in the air fryer basket.
4. Crack an egg onto each naan bread.
5. Add spinach leaves, diced tomatoes, and crumbled feta cheese evenly on top of each naan and egg.
6. Season with salt and pepper.
7. Using the Bake mode, cook the Breakfast Naan for about 8-10 minutes or until the eggs are cooked to your desired level and the naan is toasted.
8. Remove the Breakfast Naan from the air fryer.
9. Serve your Breakfast Naan hot.

Breakfast Focaccia

Prep Time: 15 minutes / Cook Time: 10 minutes
Servings: 4 / Mode: Bake

Ingredients:

- 240g All-purpose flour
- 8g Baking powder
- 3g Salt
- 180ml Lukewarm water
- 22.5ml Olive oil
- 120g Greek yoghourt

- 150g Cherry tomatoes, halved
- 100g Feta cheese, crumbled
- 15g Fresh basil leaves
- Salt and pepper to taste
- Olive oil for drizzling

Preparation Instructions:

1. In a mixing bowl, combine 240g all-purpose flour, 8g baking powder, and 3g salt.
2. Add 180ml lukewarm water, 22.5ml olive oil, and 120g Greek yogurt. Mix until a dough forms.
3. Knead the dough on a floured surface for about 5 minutes until it's smooth. Divide the dough into four portions and roll each into a thin focaccia.
4. Preheat your air fryer to 350°F .
5. Place one focaccia in the air fryer basket and cook for 5-6 minutes, flipping halfway through, or until they puff up and have golden brown spots. Repeat with the remaining focaccias.
6. While the focaccias are cooking, sauté the cherry tomatoes in a pan on the stove.
7. Spread the cooked tomatoes on the focaccias, sprinkle with 100g crumbled feta cheese, fresh basil, salt, and pepper.
8. Drizzle with a bit of olive oil if desired.
9. Serve your Breakfast Focaccia warm for a delightful morning meal.

Air-Fried Breakfast Danishes

Prep Time: 20 minutes / Cook Time: 10 minutes
Servings: 4 / Mode: Air Fry

Ingredients:

- 240g Puff pastry dough
- 60g Cream cheese
- 30g Powdered sugar
- 5ml Vanilla extract
- 60g Fruit jam or preserves (e.g., raspberry, apricot)
- 1 Egg (for egg wash)
- Powdered sugar for dusting (optional)

Preparation Instructions:

1. Roll out 240g puff pastry dough into a rectangle and cut it into four equal squares.
2. In a mixing bowl, combine 60g cream cheese, 30g powdered sugar, and 5ml vanilla extract. Mix until smooth.
3. Place a spoonful of the cream cheese mixture in the centre of each puff pastry square.
4. Add a dollop of fruit jam or preserves on top of the cream cheese mixture.
5. Fold the corners of each square towards the centre,

forming a danish shape.

6. Preheat your air fryer to 375°F.
7. Beat the egg and brush it over the danishes for a golden finish.
8. Place the danishes in the air fryer basket.
9. Air fry the danishes using the Air Fry mode for about 8-10 minutes, or until they are puffed and golden brown.
10. Optionally, dust with powdered sugar before serving.
11. Serve hot and enjoy your delightful morning meal.

Breakfast Strudel

Prep Time: 20 minutes / Cook Time: 20 minutes
Servings: 4 / Mode: Bake

Ingredients:

- 240g Puff pastry dough
- 120g Cream cheese
- 60g Powdered sugar
- 5ml Vanilla extract
- 120g Fruit jam or preserves (e.g., apple, cherry)
- 1 Egg (for egg wash)
- Powdered sugar for dusting (optional)

Preparation Instructions:

1. Roll out 240g puff pastry dough into a rectangle and cut it into four equal squares.
2. In a mixing bowl, combine 120g cream cheese, 60g powdered sugar, and 5ml vanilla extract. Mix until smooth.
3. Place a spoonful of the cream cheese mixture in the centre of each puff pastry square.
4. Add 30g of fruit jam or preserves on top of the cream cheese mixture in each square.
5. Fold the corners of each square towards the centre, forming a strudel shape.
6. Preheat your air fryer to 375°F.
7. Beat the egg and brush it over the strudels for a golden finish.
8. Place the strudels in the air fryer basket.
9. Air fry the strudels using the Bake mode for about 15-20 minutes or until they are puffed and golden brown.
10. Optionally, dust with powdered sugar before serving.
11. Serve your and enjoy hot for a wholesome breakfast experience.

Breakfast Biscuit Bombs

Prep Time: 15 minutes / Cook Time: 10 minutes
Servings: 4 / Mode: Air Fry

Ingredients:

- 240g Refrigerated biscuit dough (canned)
- 4 Cooked breakfast sausage links
- 4 Small slices of cheddar cheese
- 1 Egg (for egg wash)
- 5ml Milk

Preparation Instructions:

1. Flatten out each biscuit dough round from the can.
2. Place a cooked breakfast sausage link and a small slice of cheddar cheese in the centre of each biscuit.
3. Fold the biscuit dough around the sausage and cheese, sealing it to form a ball.
4. Preheat your air fryer to 350°F.
5. In a small bowl, whisk together 1 egg and 5ml of milk to create an egg wash.
6. Dip each biscuit bomb in the egg wash, coating it evenly.
7. Place the biscuit bombs in the air fryer basket.
8. Air fry the biscuit bombs using the Air Fry mode for about 8-10 minutes, or until they are golden brown and cooked through.
9. Serve your Breakfast Biscuit Bombs as a savoury breakfast delight.

Cinnamon Sugar Donuts

Prep Time: 15 minutes / Cook Time: 10 minutes
Servings: 4 / Mode: Air Fry

Ingredients:

- 240g Refrigerated biscuit dough (canned)
- 30g Granulated sugar
- 5g Ground cinnamon
- 30g Butter, melted

Preparation Instructions:

1. Flatten out each biscuit dough round from the can.
2. In a small bowl, combine 30g granulated sugar and 5g ground cinnamon.
3. Dip each biscuit round into the melted butter, coating it thoroughly.
4. Roll the butter-coated biscuit in the cinnamon-sugar mixture, ensuring it's evenly coated.
5. Preheat your air fryer to 350°F.
6. Place the cinnamon sugar-coated biscuits in the air fryer basket.
7. Air fry the donuts using the Air Fry mode for about 8-10 minutes or until they are golden brown and cooked through.
8. Serve your Cinnamon Sugar Donuts as a sweet breakfast treat.

Chapter 2 Snacks

Chocolate Churros

Prep Time: 20 minutes / Cook Time: 10 minutes
Servings: 4 / Mode: Air Fry

Ingredients:
- 120g All-purpose flour
- 15g Unsweetened cocoa powder
- 2.5g Baking powder
- 2.5g Salt
- 240ml Water
- 15g Granulated sugar
- 15ml Vegetable oil
- 5ml Vanilla extract
- 120g Semisweet chocolate chips
- Vegetable oil for brushing
- Cinnamon sugar (mix of ground cinnamon and granulated sugar) for coating

Preparation Instructions:
1. In a mixing bowl, combine 120g all-purpose flour, 15g unsweetened cocoa powder, 2.5g baking powder, and 2.5g salt.
2. In a saucepan, heat 240ml water, 15g granulated sugar, 15ml vegetable oil, and 5ml vanilla extract until it comes to a boil.
3. Pour the hot liquid mixture into the dry ingredients and stir until a smooth dough forms.
4. Stir in 120g semisweet chocolate chips.
5. Preheat your air fryer to 375°F.
6. Transfer the churro dough into a piping bag with a star tip.
7. Pipe strips of dough into the air fryer basket, brushing each with a bit of vegetable oil.
8. Air fry the churros using the Air Fry mode for about 8-10 minutes or until they are golden brown and cooked through.
9. While still warm, roll the churros in cinnamon sugar to coat them.
10. Serve your Chocolate Churros with a dipping sauce or enjoy them on their own.

S'mores Quesadillas

Prep Time: 15 minutes / Cook Time: 10 minutes
Servings: 4 / Mode: Air Fry

Ingredients:
- 4 Flour tortillas
- 120g Chocolate chips
- 120g Mini marshmallows
- 60g Crushed graham crackers
- Vegetable oil for brushing

Preparation Instructions:
1. Lay out four flour tortillas.
2. Sprinkle 120g chocolate chips, 120g mini marshmallows, and 60g crushed graham crackers evenly over two of the tortillas.
3. Place the remaining two tortillas on top to create quesadilla sandwiches.
4. Preheat your air fryer to 375°F.
5. Brush the outside of each quesadilla lightly with vegetable oil.
6. Place the quesadillas in the air fryer basket.
7. Air fry the quesadillas using the Air Fry mode for about 8-10 minutes or until they are golden brown and the chocolate and marshmallows are melted.
8. Remove the quesadillas from the air fryer and allow them to cool slightly before cutting into wedges.
9. Serve your sweet S'mores Quesadillas and enjoy.

Air-Fried Donuts

Prep Time: 15 minutes / Cook Time: 8 minutes
Servings: 4 / Mode: Air Fry

Ingredients:
- 240g Refrigerated biscuit dough (canned)
- 30g Granulated sugar
- 5g Ground cinnamon
- 30g Butter, melted
- 60ml Maple syrup (for dipping)

Preparation Instructions:
1. Flatten out each biscuit dough round from the can.
2. In a small bowl, combine 30g granulated sugar and 5g ground cinnamon.
3. Dip each biscuit round into the melted butter, coating it thoroughly.
4. Roll the butter-coated biscuit in the cinnamon-sugar mixture, ensuring it's evenly coated.
5. Preheat your air fryer to 350°F .
6. Place the cinnamon sugar-coated biscuits in the air fryer basket.
7. Air fry the donuts using the Air Fry mode for about 7-8 minutes or until they are golden brown and cooked through.
8. While still warm, drizzle with maple syrup or dip them for added sweetness.
9. Serve your Air-Fried Donuts as a crunchy and quick snack.

Cheese Twists

Prep Time: 10 minutes / Cook Time: 8 minutes
Servings: 4 / Mode: Air Fry

Ingredients:

- 240g Puff pastry dough
- 60g Grated Parmesan cheese
- 30g Butter, melted
- 5g Garlic powder
- 5g Dried parsley flakes
- 2.5g Salt

Preparation Instructions:

1. Roll out 240g puff pastry dough into a rectangle.
2. In a small bowl, combine 60g grated Parmesan cheese, 30g melted butter, 5g garlic powder, 5g dried parsley flakes, and 2.5g salt.
3. Spread the cheese and herb mixture evenly over the puff pastry dough.
4. Cut the dough into thin strips.
5. Preheat your air fryer to 375°F.
6. Twist each strip of dough and place it in the air fryer basket.
7. Air fry the cheese twists using the Air Fry mode for about 6-8 minutes or until they are golden brown and crispy.
8. Serve your Cheese Twists as a savoury and cheesy snack.

Fried Ravioli

Prep Time: 15 minutes / Cook Time: 10 minutes
Servings: 4 / Mode: Air Fry

Ingredients:

- 240g Fresh or frozen ravioli (meat or cheese-filled)
- 60g Bread crumbs
- 30g Grated Parmesan cheese
- 1 Egg, beaten
- Marinara sauce (for dipping)

Preparation Instructions:

1. In a shallow bowl, combine 60g bread crumbs and 30g grated Parmesan cheese.
2. Dip each ravioli into the beaten egg, allowing any excess to drip off.
3. Coat the ravioli with the breadcrumb mixture, pressing gently to adhere.
4. Preheat your air fryer to 375°F.
5. Place the breaded ravioli in the air fryer basket in a single layer, making sure they are not overcrowded.
6. Air fry the ravioli using the Air Fry mode for about 8-10 minutes or until they are golden brown and crispy.
7. Serve your Fried Ravioli hot with marinara sauce for dipping.

Lemon Poppyseed Muffin Bites

Prep Time: 10 minutes / Cook Time: 10 minutes
Servings: 4 / Mode: Bake

Ingredients:

- 120g All-purpose flour
- 30g Granulated sugar
- 5g Baking powder
- 2.5g Baking soda
- 2.5g Salt
- Zest of 1 lemon
- 60ml Lemon juice
- 60ml Milk
- 30ml Vegetable oil
- 1 Egg
- 5g Poppy seeds
- Powdered sugar for dusting (optional)

Preparation Instructions:

1. In a mixing bowl, combine 120g all-purpose flour, 30g granulated sugar, 5g baking powder, 2.5g baking soda, and 2.5g salt.
2. Add the zest of 1 lemon and 60ml lemon juice to the dry ingredients. Mix until well combined.
3. In a separate bowl, whisk together 60ml milk, 30ml vegetable oil, and 1 egg.
4. Pour the wet ingredients into the dry ingredients and stir until just combined. Do not overmix.
5. Gently fold in 5g poppy seeds into the batter.
6. Preheat your air fryer to 350°F .
7. Grease the wells of a mini muffin tin.
8. Spoon the muffin batter into the greased muffin tin, filling each well about two-thirds full.
9. Place the muffin tin in the air fryer basket
10. Bake the Lemon Poppyseed Muffin Bites using the Bake mode for about 8-10 minutes or until they are golden brown and a toothpick inserted into the centre comes out clean.
11. Optionally, dust with powdered sugar before serving.
12. Serve your Lemon Poppyseed Muffin Bites as a delicious snack or breakfast option.

Baked Camembert

Prep Time: 5 minutes / Cook Time: 15 minutes
Servings: 4 / Mode: Bake

Ingredients:

- 1 whole Camembert cheese (about 250g)
- 2-3 cloves garlic, thinly sliced
- Fresh rosemary sprigs
- 15ml Olive oil
- Bread or crackers for dipping

Preparation Instructions:

1. Preheat your air fryer to 350°F .
2. Remove any packaging from 1 whole Camembert cheese (about 250g) and place it in a small oven-safe dish or wrap it in parchment paper.
3. Score the top of the Camembert with a knife in a crisscross pattern.
4. Insert thin slices of garlic and fresh rosemary sprigs into the cuts on top of the cheese.
5. Drizzle 15ml olive oil over the Camembert.
6. Place the Camembert in the air fryer basket or dish.
7. Bake the Camembert using the Bake mode for about 12-15 minutes, or until the cheese is soft and gooey in the centre.
8. Remove the Baked Camembert from the air fryer and let it cool slightly.
9. Serve your Baked Camembert with bread or crackers for dipping.

Tempura Vegetables

Prep Time: 15 minutes / Cook Time: 10 minutes
Servings: 4 / Mode: Max Crisp

Ingredients:

- 240g Assorted vegetables (e.g., bell peppers, zucchini, sweet potato, broccoli florets)
- 120g All-purpose flour
- 2.5g Salt
- 180ml Ice-cold sparkling water
- Vegetable oil for frying
- Dipping sauce (soy sauce or tempura dipping sauce)

Preparation Instructions:

1. Cut 240g assorted vegetables into thin strips or bite-sized pieces.
2. In a mixing bowl, combine 120g all-purpose flour and 2.5g salt.
3. Gradually add 180ml ice-cold sparkling water to the flour mixture and whisk until you have a smooth batter.
4. Preheat your air fryer to the Max Crisp mode.
5. Dip the vegetable pieces into the tempura batter, ensuring they are well coated.
6. Shake off any excess batter and place the coated vegetables in the air fryer basket.
7. Lightly spray or brush the vegetables with vegetable oil.
8. Air fry the vegetables in the Max Crisp mode for about 5-7 minutes or until they are golden brown and crispy.
9. Serve your Tempura Vegetables hot with a dipping sauce of your choice.

Bruschetta

Prep Time: 15 minutes / Cook Time: 3 minutes
Servings: 4 / Mode: Bake

Ingredients:

- 4 Slices of baguette or Italian bread
- 2 Ripe tomatoes, diced
- 2 Cloves garlic, minced
- 60ml Extra-virgin olive oil
- 15g Fresh basil leaves, chopped
- Salt and pepper to taste
- Balsamic glaze (optional, for drizzling)

Preparation Instructions:

1. Preheat your air fryer to the Bake or Toast mode.
2. Place 4 slices of baguette or Italian bread in the air fryer basket.
3. Toast the bread slices for about 2-3 minutes or until they are crispy and golden brown.
4. Remove the toasted bread from the air fryer.
5. In a mixing bowl, combine diced tomatoes, minced garlic, chopped fresh basil, and 60ml extra-virgin olive oil. Season with salt and pepper to taste. Mix well.
6. Spoon the tomato and basil mixture generously onto each toasted bread slice.
7. Optionally, drizzle with balsamic glaze for added flavour.
8. Serve your Bruschetta as a delicious appetiser or snack.

Halloumi Fries

Prep Time: 10 minutes / Cook Time: 10 minutes
Servings: 4 / Mode: Max Crisp

Ingredients:

- 240g Halloumi cheese, cut into fries
- 60g All-purpose flour
- 2.5g Paprika
- Vegetable oil for spraying

Preparation Instructions:

1. Cut 240g Halloumi cheese into fries or strips.
2. In a mixing bowl, combine 60g all-purpose flour and 2.5g paprika.
3. Toss the Halloumi fries in the flour mixture, ensuring they are evenly coated.
4. Preheat your air fryer to the Max Crisp mode.
5. Place the Halloumi fries in the air fryer basket.
6. Lightly spray the Halloumi fries with vegetable oil.
7. Air fry the fries using the Max Crisp mode for about 8-10 minutes or until they are golden brown and crispy.
8. Serve your Halloumi Fries hot with your favourite dipping sauce.

Mini Corn Dogs

Prep Time: 15 minutes / Cook Time: 10 minutes
Servings: 4 / Mode: Max Crisp

Ingredients:

- 8 Mini sausages or hot dogs
- 120g Cornmeal
- 60g All-purpose flour
- 15g Granulated sugar
- 5g Baking powder
- 2.5g Salt
- 120ml Milk
- 1 Egg
- Vegetable oil for frying
- Ketchup and mustard for dipping (optional)

Preparation Instructions:

1. Insert wooden toothpicks into each mini sausage or hot dog, leaving part of the toothpick exposed for handling.
2. In a mixing bowl, combine 120g cornmeal, 60g all-purpose flour, 15g granulated sugar, 5g baking powder, and 2.5g salt.
3. In another bowl, whisk together 120ml milk and 1 egg until well combined.
4. Pour the wet ingredients into the dry ingredients and mix until you have a smooth batter.
5. Preheat your air fryer to the Max Crisp mode.
6. Dip each mini sausage into the batter, coating it evenly.
7. Place the battered mini sausages in the air fryer basket.
8. Lightly spray or brush the sausages with vegetable oil.
9. Air fry the Mini Corn Dogs in the Max Crisp mode for about 6-8 minutes or until they are golden brown and crispy.
10. Serve your Mini Corn Dogs with ketchup and mustard for dipping, if desired.

Battered Mars Bars

Prep Time: 10 minutes / Cook Time: 5 minutes
Servings: 4 / Mode: Max Crisp

Ingredients:

- 4 Mars Bars, frozen
- 120g All-purpose flour
- 60ml Milk
- 1 Egg
- 5g Baking powder
- 2.5g Salt
- Vegetable oil for frying
- Powdered sugar (optional, for dusting)

Preparation Instructions:

1. Freeze 4 Mars Bars for at least a few hours or until they are solid.
2. In a mixing bowl, combine 120g all-purpose flour, 5g baking powder, and 2.5g salt.
3. In another bowl, whisk together 60ml milk and 1 egg until well combined.
4. Preheat your air fryer to the Max Crisp mode.
5. Dip each frozen Mars Bar into the batter, coating it evenly.
6. Place the battered Mars Bars in the air fryer basket.
7. Air fry the Battered Mars Bars in the Max Crisp mode for about 4-5 minutes or until they are golden brown and the Mars Bars are melted inside.
8. Optionally, dust with powdered sugar before serving.
9. Serve your crispy Battered Mars Bars.

Bacon-Wrapped Dates

Prep Time: 10 minutes / Cook Time: 10 minutes
Servings: 4 / Mode: Max Crisp

Ingredients:

- 16 Medjool dates, pitted
- 8 Slices of bacon, cut in half
- 16 Toothpicks

Preparation Instructions:

1. Preheat your air fryer to the Max Crisp mode.
2. Wrap each pitted Medjool date with half a slice of bacon.
3. Secure each bacon-wrapped date with a toothpick.
4. Place the bacon-wrapped dates in the air fryer basket.
5. Air fry the Bacon-Wrapped Dates in the Max Crisp mode for about 8-10 minutes or until the bacon is crispy and cooked through.
6. Remove the toothpicks before serving.
7. Serve your Bacon-Wrapped Dates as a delicious appetiser or snack.

Tempura Squid Rings

Prep Time: 15 minutes / Cook Time: 10 minutes
Servings: 4 / Mode: Max Crisp

Ingredients:

- 240g Squid rings
- 120g All-purpose flour
- 2.5g Salt
- 180ml Ice-cold sparkling water
- Vegetable oil for frying
- Dipping sauce (e.g., soy sauce or tempura dipping sauce)

Preparation Instructions:

1. In a mixing bowl, combine 120g all-purpose flour and 2.5g salt.
2. Gradually add 180ml ice-cold sparkling water to the flour mixture and whisk until you have a smooth batter.
3. Preheat your air fryer to the Max Crisp mode.

4. Dip the squid rings into the tempura batter, ensuring they are well coated.
5. Shake off any excess batter and place the coated squid rings in the air fryer basket.
6. Lightly spray or brush the squid rings with vegetable oil.
7. Air fry the squid rings using the Max Crisp mode for about 5-7 minutes or until they are golden brown and crispy.
8. Serve your Tempura Squid Rings hot with your choice of dipping sauce.

Vegetable Pakoras

Prep Time: 15 minutes / Cook Time: 10 minutes
Servings: 4 / Mode: Max Crisp

Ingredients:

- 120g Mixed vegetables (e.g., sliced onions, spinach, potatoes)
- 120g Chickpea flour (besan)
- 5g Cumin seeds
- 2.5g Red chilli powder
- 2.5g Garam masala
- 2.5g Salt
- Water (as needed)
- Vegetable oil for frying

Preparation Instructions:

1. In a mixing bowl, combine 120g chickpea flour, 5g cumin seeds, 2.5g red chilli powder, 2.5g garam masala, and 2.5g salt.
2. Gradually add water to the flour mixture and whisk until you have a thick batter.
3. Add 1 cup of mixed vegetables (e.g., sliced onions, spinach, potatoes) to the batter and coat them evenly.
4. Preheat your air fryer to the Max Crisp mode.
5. Using a spoon, drop spoonfuls of the vegetable batter into the air fryer basket.
6. Lightly spray or brush the vegetable pakoras with vegetable oil.
7. Air fry the vegetable pakoras using the Max Crisp mode for about 8-10 minutes or until they are golden brown and crispy.
8. Serve your Vegetable Pakoras hot with chutney or sauce.

Macaroni and Cheese Bites

Prep Time: 20 minutes / Cook Time: 10 minutes
Servings: 4 / Mode: Max Crisp

Ingredients:

- 240g Cooked macaroni pasta
- 240g Shredded cheddar cheese
- 60ml Milk
- 1 Egg
- 60g Bread crumbs
- 30g Grated Parmesan cheese
- Cooking spray

Preparation Instructions:

1. In a mixing bowl, combine 240g cooked macaroni pasta, 240g shredded cheddar cheese, 60ml milk, and 1 egg. Mix until well combined.
2. Preheat your air fryer to the Max Crisp mode.
3. Shape the macaroni and cheese mixture into bite-sized balls.
4. In a separate bowl, combine 60g bread crumbs and 30g grated Parmesan cheese.
5. Roll each macaroni and cheese ball in the breadcrumb mixture, ensuring they are well coated.
6. Place the coated macaroni and cheese bites in the air fryer basket.
7. Lightly spray the bites with cooking spray.
8. Air fry the Macaroni and Cheese Bites using the Max Crisp mode for about 8-10 minutes or until they are golden brown and crispy.
9. Serve your Macaroni and Cheese Bites as a delightful and cheesy snack.

Bubblegum Marshmallow Treats

Prep Time: 10 minutes / Cook Time: 15 minutes
Servings: 4 / Mode: Bake

Ingredients:

- 120g Bubblegum-flavoured marshmallows
- 120g Rice cereal
- 30g Unsalted butter
- 60g Bubblegum candies (optional, for garnish)

Preparation Instructions:

1. In a microwave-safe bowl, melt 30g unsalted butter in the microwave.
2. Add 120g bubblegum-flavoured marshmallows to the melted butter and microwave in 15-second intervals, stirring each time, until the marshmallows are fully melted and smooth.
3. Quickly fold in 120g rice cereal and stir until well combined.
4. Grease a square or rectangular dish with butter or cooking spray.
5. Press the mixture evenly into the greased dish.
6. Optionally, garnish the top with crushed bubblegum candies.
7. Preheat your air fryer to the Bake mode.
8. Place the dish with the marshmallow mixture into the air fryer basket.

9. Bake the Bubblegum Marshmallow Treats using the Bake mode for about 15 minutes or until they are set and have a slightly golden top.
10. Let it cool and set for about 30 minutes.
11. Once set, cut the mixture into squares or bars.
12. Serve your Bubblegum Marshmallow Treats as a sweet and chewy snack with a twist.

Mini Blackcurrant Pies

Prep Time: 20 minutes / Cook Time: 15 minutes
Servings: 4 / Mode: Bake

Ingredients:

- 1 sheet of refrigerated pie crust (or homemade pie crust)
- 240g Blackcurrants (fresh or frozen)
- 60g Granulated sugar
- 5g Cornstarch
- 1 Egg (for egg wash)
- Powdered sugar (optional, for dusting)

Preparation Instructions:

1. Preheat your air fryer to the Bake mode.
2. In a mixing bowl, combine 240g blackcurrants, 60g granulated sugar, and 5g cornstarch. Mix until the blackcurrants are coated.
3. Roll out the pie crust and cut it into 4 smaller circles or squares.
4. Place a spoonful of the blackcurrant mixture onto each pie crust piece.
5. Fold the pie crust over the filling to create mini pies.
6. Beat 1 egg and brush it over the tops of the mini pies for a golden finish.
7. Place the mini pies in the air fryer basket.
8. Bake the Mini Blackcurrant Pies using the Bake mode for about 12-15 minutes or until the crust is golden brown and the filling is bubbling.
9. Optionally, dust with powdered sugar before serving.
10. Serve your Mini Blackcurrant Pies as a delightful and fruity dessert.

Mini Key Lime Pies

Prep Time: 15 minutes / Cook Time: 10 minutes
Servings: 4 / Mode: Bake

Ingredients:

- 1 prepared graham cracker pie crust (store-bought or homemade)
- 240ml Sweetened condensed milk
- 2 Egg yolks
- 60ml Key lime juice (freshly squeezed or bottled)
- 1 Key lime, zested
- Whipped cream for garnish (optional)

Preparation Instructions:

1. Preheat your air fryer to the Bake mode.
2. In a mixing bowl, combine 240ml sweetened condensed milk, 2 egg yolks, 60ml key lime juice, and the zest of 1 key lime. Mix until well combined.
3. Pour the key lime filling into the prepared graham cracker pie crust.
4. Place the mini key lime pies in the air fryer basket.
5. Bake the Mini Key Lime Pies using the Bake mode for about 8-10 minutes or until the filling is set and the edges of the crust are golden brown.
6. Remove the mini pies from the air fryer and let them cool.
7. Once cooled, optionally garnish with whipped cream and additional key lime zest.
8. Serve your Mini Key Lime Pies as a tangy and refreshing dessert.

Mini Eccles Cakes

Prep Time: 15 minutes / Cook Time: 10 minutes
Servings: 4 / Mode: Max Crisp

Ingredients:

- 1 sheet of puff pastry, thawed
- 120g Currants or raisins
- 30g Unsalted butter, melted
- 30g Granulated sugar
- 2.5g Ground cinnamon
- Milk (for brushing)
- Granulated sugar (for dusting)

Preparation Instructions:

1. Preheat your air fryer to the Max Crisp mode.
2. In a mixing bowl, combine 120g currants or raisins, 30g melted unsalted butter, 30g granulated sugar, and 2.5g ground cinnamon. Mix well to make the filling
3. Roll out the puff pastry sheet and cut it into 4 equal squares.
4. Place a spoonful of the currant filling in the centre of each pastry square.
5. Fold the pastry squares over to create small, square parcels. Press the edges to seal.
6. Brush the tops of the mini Eccles cakes with a little milk and sprinkle with granulated sugar.
7. Place the mini Eccles cakes in the air fryer basket.
8. Air fry the Mini Eccles Cakes using the Max Crisp mode for about 8-10 minutes or until they are golden brown and crispy.
9. Remove the cakes from the air fryer and let them cool slightly.
10. Serve your Mini Eccles Cakes as a delightful and sweet treat.

Chapter 3 Lunch

Pesto and Tomato Flatbreads

Prep Time: 15 minutes / Cook Time: 10 minutes
Servings: 4 / Mode: Bake

Ingredients:

- 2 Flatbreads
- 60ml Pesto sauce
- 2 Tomatoes, thinly sliced
- 120g Mozzarella cheese, shredded
- Fresh basil leaves for garnish
- Olive oil for drizzling
- Salt and pepper to taste

Preparation Instructions:

1. Preheat your air fryer to the Bake mode.
2. Place 2 flatbreads on a clean surface.
3. Spread 60ml of pesto sauce evenly over the flatbreads.
4. Arrange the thinly sliced tomatoes on top of the pesto.
5. Sprinkle 120g shredded mozzarella cheese over the tomatoes.
6. Season with salt and pepper to taste.
7. Transfer the prepared flatbreads to the air fryer basket.
8. Drizzle a bit of olive oil over the top.
9. Bake the Pesto and Tomato Flatbreads using the Bake mode for about 8-10 minutes or until the flatbreads are crispy and the cheese is melted and bubbly.
10. Remove from the air fryer and garnish with fresh basil leaves.
11. Slice and serve your Pesto and Tomato Flatbreads as a delicious lunch meal.

Mince and Skirlie Stuffed Bell Peppers

Prep Time: 20 minutes / Cook Time: 15 minutes
Servings: 4 / Mode: Max Crisp

Ingredients:

- 4 Bell peppers, any colour
- 240g Ground beef or minced meat
- 120g Skirlie (oatmeal and onion stuffing)
- 1 Onion, finely chopped
- 1 Garlic clove, minced
- 5g Dried mixed herbs
- Salt and pepper to taste
- Olive oil for brushing

Preparation Instructions:

1. Cut the tops off the bell peppers and remove the seeds and membranes from the inside.
2. In a skillet, heat some olive oil over medium heat.
3. Add 1 finely chopped onion and 1 minced garlic clove. Sauté until translucent.
4. Add 240g ground beef or minced meat and cook until browned.
5. Stir in 120g skirlie, 5g dried mixed herbs, salt, and pepper. Cook for a few minutes until well combined.
6. Preheat your air fryer to the Max Crisp mode.
7. Stuff the bell peppers with the mince and skirlie mixture.
8. Brush the outside of the peppers with a little olive oil.
9. Place the stuffed bell peppers in the air fryer basket.
10. Air fry the Stuffed Bell Peppers using the Max Crisp mode for about 12-15 minutes or until the peppers are tender and slightly charred.
11. Serve your Mince and Skirlie Stuffed Bell Peppers as a hearty and flavorful dish.

Samphire and Sea Beet Fritters

Prep Time: 15 minutes / Cook Time: 10 minutes
Servings: 4 / Mode: Max Crisp

Ingredients:

- 120g Samphire, chopped
- 120g Sea beet leaves, chopped
- 1 Egg
- 60g All-purpose flour
- 5g Baking powder
- 1 Garlic clove, minced
- Salt and pepper to taste
- Olive oil for frying

Preparation Instructions:

1. In a mixing bowl, combine 120g chopped samphire, 120g chopped sea beet leaves, 1 egg, 60g all-purpose flour, 5g baking powder, 1 minced garlic clove, salt, and pepper. Mix until you have a thick batter.
2. Preheat your air fryer to the Max Crisp mode.
3. Drop spoonfuls of the batter into the air fryer basket to form fritters.
4. Lightly flatten the fritters with the back of a spoon.
5. Air fry the Samphire and Sea Beet Fritters using the

Max Crisp mode for about 8-10 minutes or until they are golden brown and crispy.

6. Serve your fritters as a delightful lunch.

Venison and Redcurrant Sausage Sandwiches

Prep Time: 15 minutes / Cook Time: 10 minutes
Servings: 4 / Mode: Air Fry

Ingredients:

- 4 Venison and redcurrant sausages
- 4 Submarine or baguette rolls
- 120g Redcurrant jelly
- 1 Red onion, thinly sliced
- 30g Butter
- Salt and pepper to taste

Preparation Instructions:

1. Preheat your air fryer to the Air Fry mode.
2. Place 4 venison and redcurrant sausages in the air fryer basket.
3. Air fry the sausages for about 8-10 minutes or until they are cooked through and have a crispy exterior.
4. While the sausages are cooking, melt 30g butter in a pan over medium heat.
5. Add thinly sliced red onion to the pan and sauté until caramelised.
6. Slice the submarine or baguette rolls in half and lightly toast them.
7. Spread 120g redcurrant jelly on the toasted rolls.
8. Place a cooked venison and redcurrant sausage on each roll.
9. Top with caramelised red onions.
10. Season with salt and pepper to taste.
11. Serve your Venison and Redcurrant Sausage Sandwiches as a delicious and savoury meal.

Pheasant with Blackberry Sauce

Prep Time: 20 minutes / Cook Time: 15 minutes
Servings: 4 / Mode: Max Crisp

Ingredients:

- 4 Pheasant breasts
- 240g Blackberries
- 60g Sugar
- 60ml Red wine
- 1 Shallot, finely chopped
- 30g Butter
- Salt and pepper to taste

Preparation Instructions:

1. In a saucepan, combine 240g blackberries, 60g sugar, red wine, and finely chopped shallot.

2. Simmer the blackberry sauce over medium heat until it thickens and the blackberries break down.
3. Strain the sauce to remove any solids, leaving you with a smooth blackberry sauce. Keep warm.
4. Preheat your air fryer to the Max Crisp mode.
5. Season the pheasant breasts with salt and pepper.
6. Place the pheasant breasts in the air fryer basket.
7. Air fry the pheasant breasts for about 12-15 minutes or until they are cooked through and have a crispy exterior.
8. While the pheasant is cooking, heat the blackberry sauce and stir in 30g butter until it's melted and well incorporated.
9. Serve the cooked pheasant breasts with the blackberry sauce drizzled on top.
10. Garnish with extra blackberries if desired then serve hot for the best results.

Mini Blood Pudding Pies

Prep Time: 20 minutes / Cook Time: 15 minutes
Servings: 4 / Mode: Max Crisp

Ingredients:

- 4 Mini blood pudding pies (store-bought or homemade)
- 60ml Redcurrant jelly (for dipping)

Preparation Instructions:

1. Preheat your air fryer to the Max Crisp mode.
2. Place 4 mini blood pudding pies in the air fryer basket.
3. Air fry the mini blood pudding pies for about 10-12 minutes or until they are heated through and have a crispy crust.
4. While the pies are cooking, you can warm the redcurrant jelly in a microwave or on the stovetop for dipping.
5. Serve the Mini Blood Pudding Pies with a side of warm redcurrant jelly for dipping.

Whitebait with Aioli

Prep Time: 10 minutes / Cook Time: 10 minutes
Servings: 4 / Mode: Max Crisp

Ingredients:

- 240g Whitebait (fresh or frozen)
- 60g All-purpose flour
- 2.5g Salt
- 2.5g Paprika
- Vegetable oil for frying
- Lemon wedges for garnish
- For Aioli:
- 2 Garlic cloves, minced

- 120ml Mayonnaise
- 5ml Lemon juice
- Salt and pepper to taste

Preparation Instructions:

1. In a mixing bowl, combine 60g all-purpose flour, 2.5g salt, and 2.5g paprika.
2. Toss the whitebait in the flour mixture until they are well coated.
3. Preheat your air fryer to the Max Crisp mode.
4. Place the coated whitebait in the air fryer basket.
5. Lightly spray or brush the whitebait with vegetable oil.
6. Air fry the Whitebait using the Max Crisp mode for about 6-8 minutes or until they are crispy and golden brown.
7. While the whitebait is cooking, prepare the aioli. In a bowl, mix minced garlic, mayonnaise, lemon juice, salt, and pepper. Stir until well combined.
8. Serve the crispy Whitebait with lemon wedges and aioli for dipping.

Cheese and Onion Pasties with Branston Pickle

Prep Time: 20 minutes / Cook Time: 15 minutes
Servings: 4 / Mode: Max Crisp

Ingredients:

- 2 Sheets of puff pastry, thawed
- 240g Cheddar cheese, grated
- 1 Onion, finely chopped
- 60ml Branston Pickle
- 1 Egg (for egg wash)
- Milk (for brushing)

Preparation Instructions:

1. Preheat your air fryer to the Max Crisp mode.
2. In a mixing bowl, combine grated cheddar cheese, finely chopped onion, and Branston Pickle. Mix until well combined.
3. Roll out the puff pastry sheets and cut them into squares or rectangles.
4. Place a spoonful of the cheese and onion mixture in the centre of each pastry piece.
5. Fold the pastry over to create pasties and press the edges to seal.
6. Beat 1 egg and brush it over the tops of the pasties for a golden finish.
7. Place the pasties in the air fryer basket.
8. Lightly brush the pasties with milk.
9. Air fry the Cheese and Onion Pasties using the Max Crisp mode for about 12-15 minutes or until they are golden brown and puffed up.

10. Serve your pasties hot and crusty.

Goulash-Stuffed Bell Peppers

Prep Time: 20 minutes / Cook Time: 15 minutes
Servings: 4 / Mode: Max Crisp

Ingredients:

- 4 Bell peppers, any colour
- 240g Ground beef or minced meat
- 1 Onion, finely chopped
- 1 Garlic clove, minced
- 5g Paprika
- 240ml Tomato sauce
- Salt and pepper to taste
- Olive oil for brushing

Preparation Instructions:

1. Cut the tops off the bell peppers and remove the seeds and membranes from the inside.
2. In a skillet, heat some olive oil over medium heat.
3. Add finely chopped onion and minced garlic to the skillet. Sauté until translucent.
4. Add ground beef or minced meat and cook until browned.
5. Stir in paprika, tomato sauce, salt, and pepper. Cook for a few minutes until well combined.
6. Preheat your air fryer to the Max Crisp mode.
7. Stuff the bell peppers with the goulash mixture.
8. Brush the outside of the peppers with a little olive oil.
9. Place the stuffed bell peppers in the air fryer basket.
10. Air fry the Goulash-Stuffed Bell Peppers using the Max Crisp mode for about 12-15 minutes or until the peppers are tender and slightly charred.
11. Serve your Goulash-Stuffed Bell Peppers as a hearty and flavorful dish.

Stuffed Pigeon

Prep Time: 20 minutes / Cook Time: 20 minutes
Servings: 4 / Mode: Max Crisp

Ingredients:

- 4 Whole pigeons
- 240g Stuffing of your choice (e.g., breadcrumbs, herbs)
- 1 Onion, finely chopped
- 2 Garlic cloves, minced
- 30g Butter
- Salt and pepper to taste
- Olive oil for brushing

Preparation Instructions:

1. Preheat your air fryer to the Max Crisp mode.

2. In a skillet, melt 30g of butter over medium heat.
3. Add finely chopped onion and minced garlic to the skillet. Sauté until translucent.
4. Prepare your choice of stuffing mixture by combining breadcrumbs, herbs, sautéed onion, garlic, salt, and pepper. Mix well.
5. Carefully stuff each pigeon with the prepared stuffing mixture.
6. Brush the pigeons with a little olive oil.
7. Place the stuffed pigeons in the air fryer basket.
8. Air fry the Stuffed Pigeons using the Max Crisp mode for about 18-20 minutes or until they are cooked through and have a crispy exterior.
9. Serve your Stuffed Pigeons as a unique afternoon meal.

Welsh Leek and Caerphilly Cheese Tarts

Prep Time: 20 minutes / Cook Time: 15 minutes
Servings: 4 / Mode: Max Crisp

Ingredients:

- 2 Sheets of puff pastry, thawed
- 240g Caerphilly cheese, crumbled
- 2 Leeks, thinly sliced
- 60ml Heavy cream
- 1 Egg (for egg wash)
- Salt and pepper to taste

Preparation Instructions:

1. Preheat your air fryer to the Max Crisp mode.
2. Roll out the puff pastry sheets and cut them into squares or rectangles.
3. Place crumbled Caerphilly cheese and thinly sliced leeks on each pastry piece.
4. Drizzle heavy cream over the cheese and leeks.
5. Season with salt and pepper to taste.
6. Fold the pastry over to create tarts and press the edges to seal.
7. Beat 1 egg and brush it over the tops of the tarts for a golden finish.
8. Place the tarts in the air fryer basket.
9. Air fry the Welsh Leek and Caerphilly Cheese Tarts using the Max Crisp mode for about 12-15 minutes or until they are golden brown and puffed up.
10. Serve and enjoy your tarts hot.

Venison Sausages

Prep Time: 10 minutes / Cook Time: 10 minutes
Servings: 4 / Mode: Max Crisp

Ingredients:

- 4 Venison sausages
- Olive oil for brushing

Preparation Instructions:

1. Preheat your air fryer to the Max Crisp mode.
2. Place 4 venison sausages in the air fryer basket.
3. Brush the sausages with a little olive oil.
4. Air fry the Venison Sausages using the Max Crisp mode for about 8-10 minutes or until they are cooked through and have a crispy exterior.
5. Serve your Venison Sausages as a delicious and lean meat option.

Marmite and Cheese Toasties

Prep Time: 10 minutes / Cook Time: 10 minutes
Servings: 4 / Mode: Toast or Bake

Ingredients:

- 8 Slices of bread
- 240g Cheddar cheese, grated
- Marmite (to taste)
- Butter (for spreading)

Preparation Instructions:

1. Spread a thin layer of butter on one side of each slice of bread.
2. On the non-buttered side of 4 slices of bread, spread Marmite according to your taste preference.
3. Sprinkle grated Cheddar cheese evenly over the Marmite.
4. Place the remaining 4 slices of bread on top to create sandwiches with the buttered side facing out.
5. Preheat your air fryer to the Toast or Bake mode at around 350°F .
6. Place the assembled Marmite and Cheese Toasties in the air fryer basket.
7. Air fry the toasties using the Toast or Bake mode for about 5-7 minutes, or until they are golden brown and the cheese is melted, checking periodically to avoid overcooking.
8. Remove from the air fryer, let them cool for a minute, and then slice diagonally.
9. Serve your delicious Marmite and Cheese Toasties hot.

Battered White Pudding

Prep Time: 15 minutes / Cook Time: 10 minutes
Servings: 4 / Mode: Air Fry

Ingredients:

- 240g White pudding, sliced
- 120g All-purpose flour
- 2.5g Baking powder
- 1 Egg

- 120ml Milk
- Vegetable oil for frying

Preparation Instructions:

1. In a mixing bowl, combine 120g all-purpose flour and 2.5g baking powder.
2. In another bowl, whisk 1 egg and 120ml milk until well combined.
3. Dip each slice of white pudding into the egg and milk mixture, allowing any excess to drip off.
4. Coat the soaked white pudding slices with the flour mixture evenly.
5. Preheat your air fryer to either the Fry mode or Max Crisp mode, depending on your air fryer model.
6. Place the battered white pudding slices in the air fryer basket.
7. Air fry the Battered White Pudding for about 8-10 minutes or until they are crispy and golden brown, checking periodically to avoid overcooking.
8. Remove from the air fryer and drain on paper towels then serve hot.

Haggis and Neeps Spring Rolls

Prep Time: 20 minutes / Cook Time: 10 minutes
Servings: 4 / Mode: Air Fry

Ingredients:

- 8 Spring roll wrappers
- 240g Haggis, cooked and crumbled
- 240g Neeps (Swede or turnips), cooked and mashed
- 30g Butter
- Salt and pepper to taste
- Vegetable oil for brushing

Preparation Instructions:

1. In a skillet, melt 30g of butter over medium heat.
2. Combine the cooked and crumbled haggis with the mashed neeps in the skillet. Season with salt and pepper. Cook for a few minutes until well combined. Let it cool slightly.
3. Place a spring roll wrapper on a clean surface, with one corner facing you.
4. Spoon some of the haggis and neeps mixture onto the centre of the wrapper.
5. Fold the bottom corner over the filling, tuck in the sides, and roll it up tightly like a burrito, sealing the top corner with a bit of water to form a seal. Repeat with the remaining wrappers and filling.

6. Preheat your air fryer to the Air Fry mode at 350°F.
7. Brush the spring rolls with a little vegetable oil.
8. Place the spring rolls in the air fryer basket, leaving some space between them.
9. Air fry the Haggis and Neeps Spring Rolls using the Air Fry mode for about 8-10 minutes, or until they are golden brown and crispy.
10. Remove from the air fryer and let them cool for a minute.
11. Serve your Haggis and Neeps Springs hot and crispy.

Scotch Woodcock

Prep Time: 10 minutes / Cook Time: 10 minutes
Servings: 4 / Mode: Air Fry

Ingredients:

- 4 Slices of toast
- 4 Large eggs
- 240ml Milk
- 30g Butter
- Salt and white pepper to taste
- Ground nutmeg (optional)
- Chopped chives or parsley for garnish

Preparation Instructions:

1. In a saucepan, melt 30g of butter over low heat.
2. Stir in 240ml of milk and heat gently until it's warm but not boiling.
3. Season the milk mixture with salt, white pepper, and a pinch of ground nutmeg (if desired).
4. In a bowl, whisk the eggs together.
5. Slowly pour the egg mixture into the warm milk mixture, stirring constantly. Continue to cook gently until the mixture thickens to a creamy consistency. Remove from heat.
6. Preheat your air fryer to the Air Fry mode at 350°F.
7. Toast the slices of bread until they are lightly browned.
8. Pour the creamy scrambled eggs over the toasted slices of bread.
9. Place the prepared Scotch Woodcock in the air fryer basket.
10. Air fry the Scotch Woodcock using the Air Fry mode for about 5-7 minutes, or until they are heated through.
11. Garnish with chopped chives or parsley.
12. Enjoy your Scotch Woodcock as a flavourful dish.

Chapter 4 Dinner

Venison Medallions with Juniper Sauce

Prep Time: 20 minutes / Cook Time: 10 minutes
Servings: 2 / Mode: Max Crisp

Ingredients:

- 2 Venison medallions (about 180g each)
- Salt and black pepper to taste
- 5g Fresh rosemary leaves, minced
- 10 Juniper berries, crushed
- 15ml Olive oil
- 30ml Red wine
- 60ml Beef or game stock
- 30ml Heavy cream
- 15g Butter

Preparation Instructions:

1. Preheat your air fryer to the Max Crisp mode at 400°F.
2. Season the venison medallions with salt, black pepper, minced rosemary, and crushed juniper berries on both sides.
3. Drizzle olive oil over the medallions.
4. Place the seasoned venison medallions in the air fryer basket.
5. Air fry the Venison Medallions in the preheated air fryer for about 4-5 minutes on each side for medium-rare (adjust the time according to your desired level of doneness).
6. While the medallions are cooking, prepare the juniper sauce. In a saucepan, combine red wine and beef or game stock. Simmer over low heat until reduced by half.
7. Stir in heavy cream and continue to simmer until the sauce thickens slightly.
8. Remove the saucepan from heat and whisk in the butter until the sauce is smooth and glossy.
9. Once the venison medallions are cooked to your liking, remove them from the air fryer.
10. Serve the Venison Medallions with the Juniper Sauce drizzled over the top.

Goulash-Stuffed Bell Peppers

Prep Time: 20 minutes / Cook Time: 15 minutes
Servings: 4 / Mode: Max Crisp

Ingredients:

- 4 Bell peppers, any colour
- 240g Ground beef or minced meat
- 1 Onion, finely chopped
- 1 Garlic clove, minced
- 5g Paprika
- 240ml Tomato sauce
- Salt and pepper to taste
- Olive oil for brushing

Preparation Instructions:

1. Cut the tops off the bell peppers and remove the seeds and membranes from the inside.
2. In a skillet, heat some olive oil over medium heat.
3. Add finely chopped onion and minced garlic to the skillet. Sauté until translucent.
4. Add ground beef or minced meat and cook until browned.
5. Stir in paprika, tomato sauce, salt, and pepper. Cook for a few minutes until well combined.
6. Preheat your air fryer to the Max Crisp mode at 350°F.
7. Stuff the bell peppers with the goulash mixture.
8. Brush the outside of the peppers with a little olive oil.
9. Place the stuffed bell peppers in the air fryer basket.
10. Air fry the Goulash-Stuffed Bell Peppers using the Max Crisp mode for about 12-15 minutes or until the peppers are tender and slightly charred.
11. Serve your Goulash-Stuffed Bell Peppers hot and crispy.

Duck Confit with Cherry Gastrique

Prep Time: 20 minutes / Cook Time: 40 minutes
Servings: 2 / Mode: Max Crisp

Ingredients:

- 2 Duck leg quarters, confit
- 100g Fresh or frozen cherries
- 60ml Red wine vinegar
- 60ml Red wine
- 30g Sugar
- Salt and pepper to taste

Preparation Instructions:

1. In a saucepan, combine cherries, red wine vinegar, red wine, and sugar. Cook over medium heat until the mixture thickens into a gastrique. Season with salt and pepper. Set aside.
2. Preheat your air fryer to the Max Crisp mode at

350°F.

3. Place the duck leg quarters in the air fryer basket.
4. Air fry the Duck Confit using the Max Crisp mode for about 30-40 minutes until the skin is crispy and the duck is heated through.
5. Serve the Duck Confit with Cherry Gastrique drizzled on top.

Sweetbreads with Capers and Lemon

Prep Time: 30 minutes / Cook Time: 20 minutes
Servings: 2 / Mode: Max Crisp

Ingredients:
- 250g Sweetbreads
- Salt and black pepper to taste
- 30g All-purpose flour
- 30ml Olive oil
- 1 Lemon, sliced
- 15g Capers
- 30ml White wine
- 60ml Chicken or veal stock
- 15g Butter
- Fresh parsley for garnish

Preparation Instructions:
1. Preheat your air fryer to 400°F using the Max Crisp mode.
2. Rinse the sweetbreads under cold water and pat them dry. Season with salt and black pepper.
3. Dredge the sweetbreads in all-purpose flour to coat evenly.
4. In a skillet, heat olive oil over medium-high heat. Add the sweetbreads and cook until browned on all sides.
5. Add lemon slices and capers to the skillet. Sauté for a minute.
6. Pour in white wine and chicken or veal stock. Simmer until the liquid is reduced by half.
7. Stir in butter to create a sauce.
8. Transfer the sweetbreads and caper-lemon sauce to an oven-safe dish.
9. Place the dish in the preheated air fryer and cook using the Max Crisp mode for about 8-10 minutes or until the sweetbreads are heated through and have a crispy exterior.
10. Garnish with fresh parsley and serve the Sweetbreads with Capers and Lemon as a savoury dish.

Rabbit and Prune Tagine

Prep Time: 30 minutes / Cook Time: 1 hour 30 minutes

Servings: 4 / Mode: Roast

Ingredients:
- 1 Rabbit, cut into pieces
- 240g Prunes, pitted
- 1 Onion, chopped
- 2 Garlic cloves, minced
- 15g Fresh ginger, minced
- 5g Ground cumin
- 5g Ground coriander
- 5g Ground cinnamon
- 5g Ground paprika
- 5g Ground turmeric
- 240ml Chicken stock
- Salt and black pepper to taste
- Olive oil for drizzling

Preparation Instructions:
1. Preheat your air fryer to 350°F using the Roast mode.
2. In a large bowl, combine the rabbit pieces with chopped onion, minced garlic, minced ginger, ground cumin, ground coriander, ground cinnamon, ground paprika, ground turmeric, salt, and black pepper. Mix well.
3. Drizzle olive oil over the rabbit mixture and toss to coat.
4. Place the rabbit mixture in an oven-safe dish.
5. Roast the Rabbit and Prune Tagine in the preheated air fryer using the Roast mode for about 1 hour, turning the pieces occasionally, until the rabbit is browned and cooked through.
6. Add pitted prunes and chicken stock to the dish. Continue roasting for another 30 minutes or until the prunes are soft and the rabbit is tender.
7. Serve the Rabbit and Prune Tagine as a delightful and flavorful Moroccan-inspired dish.

Welsh Leek and Caerphilly Cheese Pie

Prep Time: 30 minutes / Cook Time: 30 minutes
Servings: 4 / Mode: Bake

Ingredients:
- 1 Sheet of puff pastry, thawed
- 240g Caerphilly cheese, crumbled
- 2 Leeks, thinly sliced
- 60ml Heavy cream
- Salt and black pepper to taste
- 1 Egg (for egg wash)

Preparation Instructions:
1. Preheat your air fryer to 375°F using the Bake

mode.

2. Roll out the puff pastry sheet and line a pie dish with it.

3. Layer half of the crumbled Caerphilly cheese on the bottom of the pastry.

4. Top with thinly sliced leeks and the remaining cheese.

5. Drizzle heavy cream over the filling. Season with salt and black pepper.

6. Place another sheet of puff pastry over the top and crimp the edges to seal the pie.

7. Beat 1 egg and brush it over the top of the pie for a golden finish.

8. Place the pie in the preheated air fryer using the Bake mode and bake for about 25-30 minutes or until the pastry is golden brown and the filling is heated through.

9. Serve the Welsh Leek and Caerphilly Cheese Pie hot for the best taste.

Crispy Duck Legs with Plum Sauce

Prep Time: 20 minutes / Cook Time: 50 minutes
Servings: 2 / Mode: Max Crisp

Ingredients:

- 2 Duck leg quarters
- Salt and black pepper to taste
- 5g Chinese five-spice powder
- 15ml Soy sauce
- 15ml Hoisin sauce
- 30ml Plum sauce
- 15ml Rice vinegar
- 15ml Honey
- 15ml Water
- 2 Green onions, chopped (for garnish)
- Sesame seeds (for garnish)

Preparation Instructions:

1. Preheat your air fryer to 375°F using the Max Crisp mode.

2. Score the duck skin and season the duck leg quarters with salt, black pepper, and Chinese five-spice powder.

3. Place the seasoned duck legs in the preheated air fryer.

4. Air fry the duck legs for about 40-45 minutes, turning them halfway through, until they are crispy and cooked through.

5. While the duck legs are cooking, prepare the plum sauce by mixing soy sauce, hoisin sauce, plum sauce, rice vinegar, honey, and water in a saucepan.

Simmer until it thickens.

6. Once the duck legs are done, remove them from the air fryer.

7. Serve the Crispy Duck Legs with Plum Sauce, garnished with chopped green onions and sesame seeds.

Venison Medallions with Sloe Gin Sauce

Prep Time: 20 minutes / Cook Time: 10 minutes
Servings: 2 / Mode: Max Crisp

Ingredients:

- 2 Venison medallions (about 180g each)
- Salt and black pepper to taste
- 5g Fresh rosemary leaves, minced
- 30ml Sloe gin
- 60ml Beef or game stock
- 30ml Heavy cream
- 15g Butter

Preparation Instructions:

1. Preheat your air fryer to 400°F using the Max Crisp mode.

2. Season the venison medallions with salt, black pepper, and minced fresh rosemary on both sides.

3. Place the seasoned venison medallions in the preheated air fryer.

4. Air fry the Venison Medallions for about 4-5 minutes on each side for medium-rare (adjust the time according to your desired level of doneness).

5. While the venison is cooking, prepare the sloe gin sauce. In a saucepan, combine sloe gin and beef or game stock. Simmer until reduced by half.

6. Stir in heavy cream and continue to simmer until the sauce thickens slightly.

7. Remove the saucepan from heat and whisk in butter until the sauce is smooth and glossy.

8. Once the venison medallions are cooked to your liking, remove them from the air fryer.

9. Serve the Venison Medallions with Sloe Gin Sauce.

Quail with Blackcurrant Sauce

Prep Time: 30 minutes / Cook Time: 25 minutes
Servings: 2 / Mode: Max Crisp

Ingredients:

- 2 Quail
- Salt and black pepper to taste
- 15ml Olive oil
- 240ml Red wine
- 60ml Blackcurrant preserves

- 30ml Balsamic vinegar
- 15g Butter

Preparation Instructions:

1. Preheat your air fryer to 375°F using the Max Crisp mode.
2. Season the quail with salt and black pepper.
3. Rub the quail with olive oil.
4. Place the seasoned quail in the preheated air fryer.
5. Air fry the quail for about 20-25 minutes, turning them halfway through, until they are golden brown and cooked through.
6. While the quail is cooking, prepare the blackcurrant sauce. In a saucepan, combine red wine, blackcurrant preserves, and balsamic vinegar. Simmer until it thickens.
7. Stir in butter to create a rich sauce.
8. Once the quail are done, remove them from the air fryer.
9. Serve the Quail with Blackcurrant Sauce, drizzled with the flavorful sauce.

Cabbage Rolls with Lamb and Barley

Prep Time: 45 minutes / Cook Time: 50 minutes
Servings: 4 / Mode: Max Crisp

Ingredients:

- 8 Large cabbage leaves
- 300g Ground lamb
- 100g Pearl barley
- 1 Onion, finely chopped
- 2 Garlic cloves, minced
- 5g Ground cumin
- 5g Ground coriander
- 5g Paprika
- 240ml Tomato sauce
- Salt and black pepper to taste
- Olive oil for brushing

Preparation Instructions:

1. Preheat your air fryer to 375°F using the Max Crisp mode.
2. In a pot of boiling water, blanch the cabbage leaves for a few minutes until they are pliable. Drain and set aside.
3. In a skillet, heat olive oil over medium heat. Add chopped onion and minced garlic. Sauté until translucent.
4. Add ground lamb and cook until browned. Drain excess fat.
5. Stir in pearl barley, ground cumin, ground coriander, paprika, tomato sauce, salt, and black

pepper. Simmer for about 20-25 minutes until the barley is cooked.
6. Place a portion of the lamb and barley mixture on each cabbage leaf. Roll up the leaves, folding in the sides as you go.
7. Brush the outside of the cabbage rolls with a little olive oil.
8. Place the cabbage rolls in the preheated air fryer.
9. Air fry the Cabbage Rolls with Lamb and Barley for about 25-30 minutes or until the cabbage is crispy and the filling is heated through.
10. Serve the cabbage rolls as a delicious and hearty dish.

Beef Tacos with Salsa Verde

Prep Time: 15 minutes / Cook Time: 15 minutes
Servings: 4 / Mode: Max Crisp

Ingredients:

- For the Beef Filling:
- 500g Ground beef
- 1 Onion, finely chopped
- 2 Garlic cloves, minced
- 5g Ground cumin
- 5g Ground chilli powder
- 240ml Salsa verde
- Salt and black pepper to taste
- Olive oil for cooking
- For Assembling:
- 8 Small flour tortillas
- 240g Shredded lettuce
- 240g Shredded cheddar cheese
- Sour cream (optional)
- Fresh cilantro leaves (for garnish)

Preparation Instructions:

1. Preheat your air fryer to 375°F using the Max Crisp mode.
2. In a skillet, heat olive oil over medium-high heat. Add chopped onion and minced garlic. Sauté until the onion becomes translucent.
3. Add ground beef to the skillet and cook until browned, breaking it apart as it cooks.
4. Season the beef with ground cumin, ground Chilli powder, salt, and black pepper. Stir to combine.
5. Pour in salsa verde and simmer for a few minutes until the mixture thickens.
6. Warm the flour tortillas in the preheated air fryer for about 1-2 minutes until they are soft and slightly crispy.
7. To assemble each taco, place a portion of the beef filling in the centre of a tortilla. Top with shredded

lettuce, shredded cheddar cheese, and a dollop of sour cream if desired.

8. Garnish with fresh cilantro leaves.
9. Serve the Beef Tacos with Salsa Verde as a delicious and satisfying dinner.

Grouse with Blackberry Sauce

Prep Time: 20 minutes / Cook Time: 30 minutes
Servings: 2 / Mode: Max Crisp

Ingredients:

- 2 Grouse
- Salt and black pepper to taste
- 15ml Olive oil
- 100g Fresh blackberries
- 60ml Red wine
- 60ml Chicken or game stock
- 15g Butter

Preparation Instructions:

1. Preheat your air fryer to 375°F using the Max Crisp mode.
2. Season the grouse with salt and black pepper.
3. Rub the grouse with olive oil.
4. Place the seasoned grouse in the preheated air fryer.
5. Air fry the Grouse for about 25-30 minutes, turning them occasionally, until they are browned and cooked through.
6. While the grouse is cooking, prepare the blackberry sauce. In a saucepan, combine fresh blackberries, red wine, and chicken or game stock. Simmer until the sauce thickens.
7. Stir in butter to create a rich sauce.
8. Once the grouse is done, remove them from the air fryer.
9. Serve the Grouse with Blackberry Sauce, drizzled with the flavorful sauce.

White Pudding with Cider Reduction

Prep Time: 10 minutes / Cook Time: 20 minutes
Servings: 2 / Mode: Max Crisp

Ingredients:

- 200g White pudding
- 60ml Apple cider
- 15g Butter
- Fresh parsley leaves (for garnish)

Preparation Instructions:

1. Preheat your air fryer to 375°F using the Max Crisp mode.
2. In a skillet, melt butter over medium heat. Add

white pudding and cook until browned on all sides.
3. Pour in apple cider and simmer until it reduces into a thick glaze.
4. Transfer the White Pudding with Cider Reduction to a serving plate.
5. Garnish with fresh parsley leaves.

Butternut Squash and Goat Cheese Galette

Prep Time: 20 minutes / Cook Time: 30 minutes
Servings: 4 / Mode: Bake

Ingredients:

- For the Galette:
- 1 Butternut squash, peeled and thinly sliced
- 100g Goat cheese, crumbled
- 5g Fresh thyme leaves
- Salt and black pepper to taste
- Olive oil for drizzling
- 1 Prepared pie crust (store-bought or homemade)
- For Assembling:
- 1 Egg, beaten (for egg wash)
- Honey (for drizzling)

Preparation Instructions:

1. Preheat your air fryer to 375°F using the Bake mode.
2. In a bowl, toss the thinly sliced butternut squash with olive oil, fresh thyme leaves, salt, and black pepper.
3. Roll out the prepared pie crust and place it on a baking sheet.
4. Arrange the seasoned butternut squash slices in the centre of the pie crust, leaving about a 2-inch border.
5. Sprinkle crumbled goat cheese over the squash.
6. Fold the edges of the pie crust over the filling to create a rustic galette.
7. Brush the edges of the galette with beaten egg for a golden crust.
8. Drizzle honey over the butternut squash.
9. Place the galette in the preheated air fryer and bake for about 25-30 minutes or until the crust is golden brown and the squash is tender.
10. Serve the Butternut Squash and Goat Cheese Galette as a delicious appealing dish.

Pigeon with Redcurrant Glaze

Prep Time: 15 minutes / Cook Time: 25 minutes
Servings: 2 / Mode: Max Crisp

Ingredients:

- 2 Pigeon breasts
- Salt and black pepper to taste

- 15ml Olive oil
- 60ml Redcurrant jelly
- 30ml Red wine
- Fresh thyme sprigs (for garnish)

Preparation Instructions:

1. Preheat your air fryer to 375°F using the Max Crisp mode.
2. Season the pigeon breasts with salt and black pepper.
3. Heat olive oil in a skillet over medium-high heat. Add pigeon breasts and sear until browned on both sides.
4. In a small saucepan, combine redcurrant jelly and red wine. Heat over low heat, stirring until the jelly melts and the mixture thickens into a glaze.
5. Brush the pigeon breasts with the redcurrant glaze.
6. Transfer the pigeon breasts to the preheated air fryer and cook for about 10-12 minutes until they reach your desired level of doneness.
7. Brush with more redcurrant glaze during cooking.
8. Serve the Pigeon with Redcurrant Glaze, garnished with fresh thyme sprigs.

Parsnip and Sage Ravioli

Prep Time: 30 minutes / Cook Time: 15 minutes
Servings: 2 / Mode: Air Fry

Ingredients:

- 200g Parsnip and sage ravioli
- 15g Butter
- Fresh sage leaves (for garnish)
- Grated Parmesan cheese (for serving)

Preparation Instructions:

1. Preheat your air fryer to 375°F using the Air Fry mode.
2. In a skillet, melt butter over medium heat.
3. Add parsnip and sage ravioli to the skillet and cook until they are crispy and golden brown on the outside, about 10-12 minutes.
4. Transfer the ravioli to a serving plate.
5. Garnish with fresh sage leaves and a sprinkle of grated Parmesan cheese.
6. Serve the Parsnip and Sage Ravioli as a delightful and quick pasta dish.

Pheasant Breast with Cranberry Sauce

Prep Time: 15 minutes / Cook Time: 20 minutes
Servings: 2 / Mode: Bake

Ingredients:

- 2 Pheasant breasts

- Salt and black pepper to taste
- 15ml Olive oil
- 120ml Cranberry sauce
- 30ml Red wine
- Fresh rosemary sprigs (for garnish)

Preparation Instructions:

1. Preheat your air fryer to 375°F using the Bake mode.
2. Season the pheasant breasts with salt and black pepper.
3. Heat olive oil in a skillet over medium-high heat. Add pheasant breasts and sear until browned on both sides.
4. In a small saucepan, combine cranberry sauce and red wine. Heat over low heat, stirring until the sauce is warmed through.
5. Brush the pheasant breasts with the cranberry sauce.
6. Transfer the pheasant breasts to the preheated air fryer and bake for about 8-10 minutes until they reach your desired level of doneness.
7. Brush with more cranberry sauce during baking.
8. Serve the Pheasant Breast with Cranberry Sauce, garnished with fresh rosemary sprigs.

Spaghetti Carbonara

Prep Time: 15 minutes / Cook Time: 15 minutes
Servings: 4 / Mode: Air Fry

Ingredients:

- 400g Spaghetti
- 200g Pancetta or guanciale, diced
- 3 Large eggs
- 100g Grated Pecorino Romano cheese
- 50g Grated Parmesan cheese
- 2 Garlic cloves, minced
- Freshly ground black pepper, to taste
- Chopped fresh parsley (for garnish)

Preparation Instructions:

1. Preheat your air fryer to 375°F using the Air Fry mode.
2. In a large pot of boiling salted water, cook the spaghetti until al dente. Drain and set aside.
3. While the spaghetti is cooking, heat a skillet over medium heat. Add the diced pancetta or guanciale and cook until it's crispy and golden brown.
4. In a mixing bowl, whisk together the eggs, grated Pecorino Romano cheese, grated Parmesan cheese, minced garlic, and freshly ground black pepper.
5. Toss the cooked spaghetti with the crispy pancetta or guanciale in the skillet.

6. Remove the skillet from the heat, and quickly pour the egg and cheese mixture over the pasta. Toss to combine, and the heat from the pasta will create a creamy sauce.
7. Transfer the Spaghetti Carbonara to a serving platter or individual plates.
8. Garnish with chopped fresh parsley.
9. Serve immediately and enjoy your delicious homemade Spaghetti Carbonara!

Oysters Rockefeller

Prep Time: 20 minutes / Cook Time: 15 minutes
Servings: 4 / Mode: Roast

Ingredients:

- 12 Fresh oysters, shucked
- 60g Fresh spinach, chopped
- 30g Fresh parsley leaves
- 15g Fresh tarragon leaves
- 2 Garlic cloves, minced
- 60g Bread crumbs
- 60g Grated Parmesan cheese
- 60ml Heavy cream
- Salt and black pepper to taste
- Lemon wedges (for garnish)

Preparation Instructions:

1. Preheat your air fryer to 350°F using the Roast mode.
2. In a food processor, combine chopped spinach, fresh parsley leaves, fresh tarragon leaves, minced garlic, bread crumbs, grated Parmesan cheese, and heavy cream. Blend until you have a smooth mixture.
3. Season the mixture with salt and black pepper to taste.
4. Place shucked oysters on a baking sheet.
5. Spoon the spinach and herb mixture over each oyster.
6. Roast the Oysters Rockefeller in the preheated air fryer for about 10-12 minutes until they are bubbling and golden brown.
7. Serve the Oysters Rockefeller with lemon wedges for garnish.

Rabbit Fricassee

Prep Time: 20 minutes / Cook Time: 45 minutes
Servings: 4 / Mode: Roast

Ingredients:

- 1 Rabbit, cut into serving pieces
- Salt and black pepper to taste
- 30ml Olive oil
- 1 Onion, chopped
- 2 Carrots, chopped
- 2 Celery stalks, chopped
- 2 Garlic cloves, minced
- 240ml Dry white wine
- 240ml Chicken broth
- 2 Bay leaves
- 5g Fresh thyme leaves
- 5g Fresh rosemary leaves
- 120ml Heavy cream
- Fresh parsley leaves (for garnish)

Preparation Instructions:

1. Preheat your air fryer to 375°F using the Roast mode.
2. Season rabbit pieces with salt and black pepper.
3. In a large skillet, heat olive oil over medium-high heat. Add rabbit pieces and brown them on all sides. Remove and set aside.
4. In the same skillet, add chopped onion, carrots, celery, and minced garlic. Sauté until the vegetables are tender.
5. Return the rabbit to the skillet. Pour in dry white wine and chicken broth.
6. Add bay leaves, fresh thyme leaves, and fresh rosemary leaves. Stir to combine.
7. Cover the skillet and place it in the preheated air fryer using the Roast mode. Cook for about 30-35 minutes until the rabbit is tender.
8. Stir in heavy cream and cook for an additional 10 minutes until the sauce thickens.
9. Serve the Rabbit Fricassee, garnished with fresh parsley leaves.

Vegetarian Halloumi and Beetroot Stacks

Prep Time: 15 minutes / Cook Time: 10 minutes
Servings: 2 / Mode: Air Fry

Ingredients:

- 200g Halloumi cheese, sliced
- 2 Medium beetroots, cooked and sliced
- 30ml Balsamic glaze
- Fresh basil leaves (for garnish)

Preparation Instructions:

1. Preheat your air fryer to 375°F using the Air Fry mode.
2. Place the halloumi cheese slices in the air fryer basket and cook for about 4-5 minutes until they are golden brown and crispy.
3. Remove the halloumi slices from the air fryer.
4. Assemble the Vegetarian Halloumi and Beetroot

Stacks by layering halloumi slices and cooked beetroot slices.

5. Drizzle with balsamic glaze and garnish with fresh basil leaves.
6. Serve and enjoy your delightful Halloumi and Beetroot Stacks.

Stuffed Quail with Chestnut Stuffing

Prep Time: 30 minutes / Cook Time: 35 minutes
Servings: 4 / Mode: Roast

Ingredients:

- 4 Quails, cleaned and patted dry
- Salt and black pepper to taste
- 100g Chestnuts, roasted and chopped
- 30g Bread crumbs
- 30g Onion, finely chopped
- 30g Celery, finely chopped
- 30g Butter
- 5g Fresh thyme leaves
- 5g Fresh rosemary leaves
- 120ml Chicken broth
- 30ml Dry white wine
- 30ml Olive oil

Preparation Instructions:

1. Preheat your air fryer to 375°F using the Roast mode.
2. In a skillet, melt butter over medium heat. Add chopped onion and celery, and sauté until they are soft.
3. Stir in chestnuts, bread crumbs, fresh thyme leaves, and fresh rosemary leaves. Cook for another 2-3 minutes.
4. Season the quails with salt and black pepper. Stuff each quail with the chestnut stuffing mixture.
5. In a separate skillet, heat olive oil over medium-high heat. Add the stuffed quails and sear until they are browned on all sides.
6. Place the seared quails in the preheated air fryer using the Roast mode. Cook for about 25-30 minutes until they are cooked through.
7. While the quails are cooking, deglaze the skillet with dry white wine and chicken broth, scraping up any browned bits.
8. Serve the Stuffed Quail with Chestnut Stuffing, drizzled with the pan sauce.

Blackberry-Glazed Duck Breast

Prep Time: 10 minutes / Cook Time: 20 minutes
Servings: 2 / Mode: Roast

Ingredients:

- 2 Duck breasts
- Salt and black pepper to taste
- 60g Blackberry jam
- 30ml Balsamic vinegar
- 30ml Red wine
- 15ml Olive oil

Preparation Instructions:

1. Preheat your air fryer to 375°F using the Roast mode.
2. Season duck breasts with salt and black pepper.
3. In a small saucepan, combine blackberry jam, balsamic vinegar, and red wine. Heat over low heat, stirring until the jam is melted and the mixture is smooth.
4. Heat olive oil in a skillet over medium-high heat. Add duck breasts, skin side down, and sear until the skin is crispy and browned.
5. Flip the duck breasts and brush with the blackberry glaze.
6. Transfer the duck breasts to the preheated air fryer using the Roast mode. Cook for about 10-12 minutes until they reach your desired level of doneness.
7. Brush with more blackberry glaze during cooking.
8. Serve the Blackberry-Glazed Duck Breast, sliced, and drizzle with additional glaze.

Gourmet Air-Fried Mushy Pea Risotto

Prep Time: 10 minutes / Cook Time: 20 minutes
Servings: 2 / Mode: Air Fry

Ingredients:

- 200g Arborio rice
- 500ml Vegetable broth, hot
- 150g Frozen peas
- 30g Grated Parmesan cheese
- 1 Small onion, finely chopped
- 1 Garlic clove, minced
- 60ml Dry white wine
- 15ml Olive oil
- Salt and black pepper to taste

Preparation Instructions:

1. Preheat your air fryer to 375°F using the Air Fry mode.
2. In a skillet, heat olive oil over medium heat. Add chopped onion and minced garlic. Sauté until they are soft.
3. Stir in Arborio rice and cook for another 2-3

minutes until the rice is translucent.

4. Pour in dry white wine and cook until it's mostly absorbed.
5. Begin adding hot vegetable broth, one ladle at a time, stirring constantly and allowing each addition to be absorbed before adding more. Continue until the rice is creamy and cooked to your desired consistency.
6. Stir in frozen peas and grated Parmesan cheese. Cook for an additional 2-3 minutes until the peas are heated through.
7. Season with salt and black pepper to taste.
8. Serve the Gourmet Air-Fried Mushy Pea Risotto hot for the best taste.

Jerk Chicken Wings with Pineapple Salsa

Prep Time: 15 minutes / Cook Time: 20 minutes
Servings: 4 / Mode: Air Fry

Ingredients:

- For Jerk Chicken Wings:
- 500g Chicken wings
- 30ml Olive oil
- 30g Jerk seasoning
- Salt and black pepper to taste
- For Pineapple Salsa:
- 1 Fresh pineapple, diced
- 1 Red bell pepper, diced
- 1 Red onion, finely chopped
- 15g Fresh cilantro leaves, chopped
- Juice of 1 lime
- Salt and black pepper to taste

Preparation Instructions:

1. Preheat your air fryer to 375°F using the Air Fry mode.
2. In a bowl, toss chicken wings with olive oil, jerk seasoning, salt, and black pepper until well coated.
3. Place the seasoned chicken wings in the air fryer basket and cook for about 18-20 minutes until they are crispy and cooked through, turning them halfway through cooking.
4. While the chicken wings are cooking, prepare the pineapple salsa by combining diced pineapple, diced red bell pepper, finely chopped red onion, chopped cilantro leaves, lime juice, salt, and black pepper in a separate bowl. Mix well.
5. Serve the Jerk Chicken Wings with Pineapple Salsa for a burst of Caribbean flavour.

Game Terrine with Cranberry Compote

Prep Time: 30 minutes / Cook Time: 55 minutes (plus cooling time)
Servings: 6 / Mode: Roast

Ingredients:

- For Game Terrine:
- 300g Mixed game meat (such as venison, pheasant, and rabbit), minced
- 100g Pork fatback, minced
- 1 Small onion, finely chopped
- 1 Garlic clove, minced
- 30ml Dry red wine
- 5g Fresh thyme leaves
- 5g Fresh rosemary leaves
- Salt and black pepper to taste
- For Cranberry Compote:
- 150g Fresh cranberries
- 60g Sugar
- 60ml Water
- Zest and juice of 1 orange

Preparation Instructions:

1. Preheat your air fryer to 375°F using the Roast mode.
2. In a bowl, combine minced game meat, minced pork fatback, finely chopped onion, minced garlic, dry red wine, fresh thyme leaves, fresh rosemary leaves, salt, and black pepper. Mix well.
3. Line a loaf pan with plastic wrap. Press the game mixture into the pan, packing it tightly.
4. Cover the top with plastic wrap and place the loaf pan in the preheated air fryer. Roast for about 50-60 minutes until the terrine is firm and cooked through.
5. While the terrine is cooling, prepare the cranberry compote by combining fresh cranberries, sugar, water, orange zest, and orange juice in a saucepan. Simmer until the cranberries burst and the mixture thickens.
6. Once the terrine has cooled, remove it from the pan, slice it, and serve with the cranberry compote.

Margherita Pizza

Prep Time: 15 minutes / Cook Time: 10 minutes
Servings: 2 / Mode: Bake

Ingredients:

- For Pizza Dough:
- 200g All-purpose flour
- 5g Active dry yeast

- 5g Sugar
- 2.5g Salt
- 120ml Lukewarm water
- 15ml Olive oil
- For Topping:
- 120ml Tomato sauce
- 150g Fresh mozzarella cheese, sliced
- Fresh basil leaves
- Salt and black pepper to taste
- Olive oil (for drizzling)

Preparation Instructions:

1. Preheat your air fryer to 375°F using the Bake mode.
2. In a small bowl, combine lukewarm water, active dry yeast, and sugar. Let it sit for about 5 minutes until it becomes frothy.
3. In a mixing bowl, combine all-purpose flour and salt. Pour in the yeast mixture and olive oil. Mix until a dough forms.
4. Knead the dough on a floured surface for about 5 minutes until it's smooth. Divide the dough into two portions.
5. Roll out each portion into a thin pizza crust.
6. Place one pizza crust in the preheated air fryer using the Bake mode. Cook for about 5 minutes or until it becomes slightly firm.
7. Remove the partially cooked pizza crust and spread tomato sauce over it. Arrange fresh mozzarella slices on top.
8. Return the pizza to the air fryer and continue baking for an additional 3-5 minutes until the crust is crispy, the cheese is melted, and the edges are golden brown.
9. Remove the Margherita Pizza from the air fryer, garnish with fresh basil leaves, season with salt and black pepper to taste, and drizzle with olive oil.
10. Slice and serve your homemade Margherita Pizza.

Stuffed Wood Pigeon

Prep Time: 30 minutes / Cook Time: 30 minutes
Servings: 2 / Mode: Roast

Ingredients:

- For Stuffed Wood Pigeon:
- 2 Wood pigeons, cleaned and dressed
- 100g Sausage meat
- 50g Onion, finely chopped
- 50g Celery, finely chopped
- 50g Carrot, finely chopped
- 2 Garlic cloves, minced
- 5g Fresh thyme leaves

- 30ml Red wine
- 15ml Olive oil
- Salt and black pepper to taste

Preparation Instructions:

1. Preheat your air fryer to 375°F using the Roast mode.
2. In a skillet, heat olive oil over medium heat. Add finely chopped onion, celery, carrot, and minced garlic. Sauté until they are soft.
3. Stir in sausage meat and cook until it's browned.
4. Add fresh thyme leaves, red wine, salt, and black pepper. Cook for another 2-3 minutes.
5. Stuff the cleaned wood pigeons with the sausage mixture.
6. Place the stuffed wood pigeons in the preheated air fryer using the Roast mode. Cook for about 25-30 minutes until they are cooked through and have a crispy skin.
7. Serve the Stuffed Wood Pigeon for a hearty night dish.

Welsh Leek and Caerphilly Cheese Soufflé

Prep Time: 20 minutes / Cook Time: 25 minutes
Servings: 2 / Mode: Bake

Ingredients:

- 100g Caerphilly cheese, grated
- 2 Large leeks, finely sliced
- 30g Butter
- 30g All-purpose flour
- 240ml Milk
- 4 Egg yolks
- 5 Egg whites
- Salt and black pepper to taste

Preparation Instructions:

1. Preheat your air fryer to 375°F using the Bake mode.
2. In a skillet, melt butter over medium heat. Add finely sliced leeks and cook until they are soft.
3. Stir in all-purpose flour and cook for another 2 minutes.
4. Gradually add milk, stirring constantly, until the mixture thickens.
5. Remove from heat and let it cool slightly. Stir in grated Caerphilly cheese, egg yolks, salt, and black pepper.
6. In a separate bowl, beat egg whites until stiff peaks form.
7. Gently fold the egg whites into the cheese and leek mixture.

8 Pour the soufflé mixture into ramekins or a baking dish.

9. Place the ramekins or baking dish in the preheated air fryer using the Bake mode. Cook for about 20-25 minutes until the soufflé is puffed and golden brown.

10. Serve the Welsh Leek and Caerphilly Cheese Soufflé immediately.

Wild Mushroom and Chestnut Pie

Prep Time: 30 minutes / Cook Time: 40 minutes
Servings: 4 / Mode: Bake

Ingredients:

- 250g Mixed wild mushrooms, cleaned and sliced
- 150g Cooked chestnuts, roughly chopped
- 1 Onion, finely chopped
- 2 Garlic cloves, minced
- 240ml Vegetable broth
- 50ml Dry white wine
- 30ml Olive oil
- 5g Fresh thyme leaves
- Salt and black pepper to taste
- 1 Sheet of puff pastry
- 1 Egg (for egg wash)

Preparation Instructions:

1. Preheat your air fryer to 375°F using the Bake mode.

2. In a skillet, heat olive oil over medium heat. Add finely chopped onion and minced garlic. Sauté until they are soft.

3. Add sliced wild mushrooms and cook until they are tender.

4. Stir in cooked chestnuts, fresh thyme leaves, dry white wine, salt, and black pepper. Cook for another 2-3 minutes.

5. Pour in vegetable broth and simmer until the mixture thickens. Remove from heat.

6. Roll out the puff pastry sheet and cut it into pieces to cover individual pie dishes or one large pie dish.

7. Spoon the mushroom and chestnut mixture into the pie dish(es).

8. Place the pie dish(es) in the preheated air fryer using the Bake mode. Cook for about 20-25 minutes until the pastry is golden brown.

9. Before serving, brush the pastry with egg wash for a shiny finish.

10. Serve the Wild Mushroom and Chestnut Pie for a delicious vegetarian dish.

Spaghetti Aglio e Olio

Prep Time: 10 minutes / Cook Time: 20 minutes
Servings: 4 / Mode: Air Fry

Ingredients:

- 400g spaghetti
- 4-6 cloves of garlic, thinly sliced
- 1/2 teaspoon red pepper flakes (adjust to taste)
- 120ml extra-virgin olive oil
- Salt, to taste
- Freshly ground black pepper, to taste
- Fresh parsley leaves, chopped, for garnish
- Grated Parmesan cheese (optional), for serving

Preparation Instructions:

1. Preheat your dual zone air fryer to 375°F using the Air Fry mode.

2. Bring a large pot of salted water to a boil. Cook the spaghetti according to the package instructions until al dente. Reserve about 240ml (1 cup) of pasta cooking water, then drain the spaghetti.

3. While the pasta is cooking, heat the extra-virgin olive oil in a large skillet over low heat. Add the sliced garlic and red pepper flakes. Cook gently, stirring occasionally, for about 5-7 minutes or until the garlic becomes fragrant and just begins to turn golden. Be careful not to burn the garlic.

4. Remove the skillet from heat and let it cool slightly.

5. Once the spaghetti is cooked and drained, return the skillet with the garlic and oil to low heat. Add the cooked spaghetti to the skillet and toss to coat the pasta with the garlic-infused oil. If the pasta seems dry, add some of the reserved pasta cooking water to create a silky sauce.

6. Season the spaghetti with salt and freshly ground black pepper, adjusting to taste.

7. Serve the Spaghetti Aglio e Olio hot, garnished with freshly chopped parsley and grated Parmesan cheese if desired.

Vegetarian caramelised Onion and Goats' Cheese Tartlets

Prep Time: 20 minutes / Cook Time: 20 minutes
Servings: 4 / Mode: Bake

Ingredients:

- 1 Sheet of puff pastry
- 2 Large onions, thinly sliced
- 30g Butter
- 30ml Balsamic vinegar
- 100g Goats' cheese, crumbled
- Fresh thyme leaves (for garnish)

- Salt and black pepper to taste

Preparation Instructions:

1. Preheat your air fryer to 375°F using the Bake mode.
2. In a skillet, melt butter over medium heat. Add thinly sliced onions and cook until they are caramelised, about 15-20 minutes.
3. Stir in balsamic vinegar and continue to cook for another 2 minutes until the vinegar is absorbed. Season with salt and black pepper.
4. Roll out the puff pastry sheet and cut it into individual tartlet-sized pieces.
5. Place the puff pastry tartlets in the preheated air fryer using the Bake mode. Cook for about 5 minutes until they become slightly firm.
6. Remove the tartlets from the air fryer and spread caramelised onions on each one.
7. Top with crumbled goats' cheese.
8. Return the tartlets to the air fryer and continue baking for another 10-15 minutes until the pastry is golden brown and the cheese is melted.
9. Garnish with fresh thyme leaves and serve your delicious Vegetarian caramelised Onion and Goats' Cheese Tartlets hot for the best taste.

Vegetarian Mushroom and Leek Pithiviers

Prep Time: 30 minutes / Cook Time: 25 minutes
Servings: 4 / Mode: Bake

Ingredients:

- 2 Sheets of puff pastry
- 250g Mixed mushrooms, sliced
- 2 Leeks, finely chopped
- 2 Garlic cloves, minced
- 30g Butter
- 240ml Vegetable broth
- 60ml Dry white wine
- 5g Fresh thyme leaves
- Salt and black pepper to taste
- 1 Egg (for egg wash)

Preparation Instructions:

1. Preheat your air fryer to 375°F using the Bake mode.
2. In a skillet, melt butter over medium heat. Add finely chopped leeks and minced garlic. Sauté until they are soft.
3. Stir in sliced mushrooms and cook until they are tender.
4. Pour in dry white wine and vegetable broth. Add fresh thyme leaves, salt, and black pepper. Simmer until the mixture thickens.

5. Roll out the puff pastry sheets and cut them into large circles.
6. Place one pastry circle on the bottom, spoon the mushroom and leek mixture onto it, leaving a border around the edges.
7. Cover with another pastry circle, pressing the edges to seal. Brush the top with egg wash for a golden finish.
8. Place the pithiviers in the preheated air fryer using the Bake mode. Cook for about 20-25 minutes until the pastry is puffed and golden brown.
9. Serve your Vegetarian Mushroom and Leek Pithiviers hot and crusty.

Black Pudding and caramelised Apple Wraps

Prep Time: 15 minutes / Cook Time: 15 minutes
Servings: 4 / Mode: Air Fry

Ingredients:

- 4 slices of black pudding (approximately 200g)
- 2 apples, cored and sliced
- 2 tablespoons brown sugar
- 2 tablespoons unsalted butter
- 4 slices of streaky bacon
- Fresh thyme leaves (for garnish)
- Salt and black pepper, to taste

Preparation Instructions:

1. Preheat your dual zone air fryer to 375°F using the Air Fry mode.
2. Wrap each slice of black pudding with a slice of streaky bacon.
3. Heat a skillet over medium heat. Add the wrapped black pudding slices and cook for about 5-7 minutes on each side until the bacon is crispy and the black pudding is heated through. Remove from the skillet and set aside.
4. In the same skillet, add the unsalted butter and brown sugar. Stir until the sugar has dissolved.
5. Add the sliced apples to the skillet and cook, stirring occasionally, for about 5 minutes or until the apples are tender and caramelised. Season with a pinch of salt and black pepper.
6. Place the bacon-wrapped black pudding slices in the preheated air fryer using the Air Fry mode. Cook for an additional 5 minutes until they become crispy.
7. To serve, place a caramelised apple slice on a plate and top it with a slice of bacon-wrapped black pudding. Garnish with fresh thyme leaves.
8. Enjoy your Black Pudding and caramelised Apple Wraps.

Chapter 5 Vegetable and Vegetarian

Stuffed Acorn Squash with Quinoa and Chickpeas

Prep Time: 20 minutes / Cook Time: 45 minutes
Servings: 4 / Mode: Roast

Ingredients:

- 2 acorn squash, halved and seeds removed
- 200g quinoa
- 500ml vegetable broth
- 1 can (15 oz) chickpeas, drained and rinsed
- 1 red bell pepper, diced
- 1 red onion, diced
- 2 cloves garlic, minced
- 30ml olive oil
- 5g ground cumin
- 2.5g ground cinnamon
- Salt and pepper to taste
- Fresh parsley (for garnish)

Preparation Instructions:

1. Preheat your dual zone air fryer to 375°F using the Roast mode.
2. Place the halved acorn squash in the air fryer basket, cut side up. Drizzle with olive oil, sprinkle with salt and pepper, and roast for about 35-40 minutes, or until the squash is tender and slightly caramelised.
3. While the squash is roasting, rinse the quinoa under cold water. In a saucepan, combine quinoa and vegetable broth. Bring to a boil, then reduce heat, cover, and simmer for about 15-20 minutes, or until the quinoa is cooked and the liquid is absorbed.
4. In a separate pan, heat olive oil over medium heat. Add diced onion and red bell pepper and sauté for about 3-4 minutes until softened. Add minced garlic and cook for another minute.
5. Add cooked quinoa, chickpeas, ground cumin, ground cinnamon, salt, and pepper to the pan. Stir to combine and cook for a few more minutes until heated through.
6. Once the acorn squash is roasted, remove them from the air fryer and stuff each squash half with the quinoa and chickpea mixture.
7. Garnish with fresh parsley and serve your delicious Stuffed Acorn Squash with Quinoa and Chickpeas.

Broccoli and Cheddar-Stuffed Sweet Potatoes

Prep Time: 10 minutes / Cook Time: 45 minutes
Servings: 4 / Mode: Bake

Ingredients:

- 4 sweet potatoes
- 160g broccoli florets, steamed and chopped
- 180g shredded cheddar cheese
- 120ml sour cream
- 30g unsalted butter
- Salt and pepper to taste
- Fresh chives (for garnish)

Preparation Instructions:

1. Preheat your dual zone air fryer to 375°F using the Bake mode.
2. Wash and scrub sweet potatoes. Pierce them with a fork in a few places.
3. Place the sweet potatoes in the air fryer basket and bake for about 40-45 minutes, or until they are tender.
4. While the sweet potatoes are baking, steam the broccoli florets until they are tender, then chop them.
5. Once the sweet potatoes are done, remove them from the air fryer and let them cool slightly.
6. Cut a slit in the top of each sweet potato and gently fluff the flesh with a fork.
7. Divide the chopped broccoli and shredded cheddar cheese evenly among the sweet potatoes, placing them in the slit.
8. Top each sweet potato with a dollop of sour cream and a pat of butter.
9. Season with salt and pepper, garnish with fresh chives, and serve your delicious Broccoli and Cheddar-Stuffed Sweet Potatoes.

Spicy Cauliflower "Wings" with Blue Cheese Dressing

Prep Time: 15 minutes / Cook Time: 15 minutes
Servings: 4 / Mode: Air Fry

Ingredients:

- 1 head cauliflower, cut into florets
- 120g all-purpose flour
- 240ml water
- 5g garlic powder
- 2.5g paprika
- 2.5g cayenne pepper (adjust for spiciness)

- Salt and pepper to taste
- Cooking spray
- Blue cheese dressing (for dipping)

Preparation Instructions:

1. Preheat your dual zone air fryer to 375°F using the Air Fry mode.
2. In a bowl, whisk together all-purpose flour, water, garlic powder, paprika, cayenne pepper, salt, and pepper to create a batter.
3. Dip cauliflower florets into the batter, ensuring they are coated evenly.
4. Place the battered cauliflower florets in the air fryer basket, leaving space between each piece. You may need to cook them in batches.
5. Air fry for about 10-15 minutes, flipping halfway through, or until the cauliflower is golden brown and crispy.
6. Remove the cauliflower "wings" from the air fryer and serve hot with blue cheese dressing for dipping.

Stuffed Sweet Potatoes with Black Beans and Avocado

Prep Time: 15 minutes / Cook Time: 45 minutes
Servings: 4 / Mode: Roast

Ingredients:

- 4 medium sweet potatoes
- 1 can (15 oz) black beans, drained and rinsed
- 2 avocados, diced
- 120g corn kernels (fresh or frozen)
- 1 red onion, finely chopped
- 2 cloves garlic, minced
- 30ml olive oil
- Juice of 1 lime
- 5g ground cumin
- Salt and pepper to taste
- Fresh cilantro (for garnish)

Preparation Instructions:

1. Preheat your dual zone air fryer to 375°F using the Roast mode.
2. Wash and scrub sweet potatoes. Pierce them with a fork in a few places.
3. Place the sweet potatoes in the air fryer basket and roast for about 40-45 minutes, or until they are tender.
4. While the sweet potatoes are roasting, heat olive oil in a skillet over medium heat. Add finely chopped red onion and minced garlic. Sauté for about 3-4 minutes until softened.
5. Add corn kernels and ground cumin to the skillet. Cook for an additional 2-3 minutes until the corn is heated through.

6. Stir in the drained black beans and cook for another 2-3 minutes. Season with salt and pepper.
7. Remove the sweet potatoes from the air fryer when done. Slice each sweet potato open and fluff the flesh with a fork.
8. Top each sweet potato with the black bean and corn mixture, diced avocado, and a drizzle of lime juice.
9. Garnish with fresh cilantro and serve your delicious Stuffed Sweet Potatoes with Black Beans and Avocado.

Spaghetti Squash with Pesto and Cherry Tomatoes

Prep Time: 15 minutes / Cook Time: 30 minutes
Servings: 4 / Mode: Roast

Ingredients:

- 1 medium spaghetti squash
- 240g cherry tomatoes, halved
- 60ml pesto sauce (store-bought or homemade)
- 30ml olive oil
- Salt and pepper to taste
- Fresh basil leaves (for garnish)
- Grated Parmesan cheese (optional)

Preparation Instructions:

1. Preheat your dual zone air fryer to 375°F using the Roast mode.
2. Cut the spaghetti squash in half lengthwise and scoop out the seeds.
3. Place the spaghetti squash halves in the air fryer basket, cut side up. Drizzle with olive oil and season with salt and pepper.
4. Roast the squash for about 25-30 minutes, or until the flesh is tender and easily shreds into "spaghetti" with a fork.
5. While the squash is roasting, halve the cherry tomatoes.
6. When the squash is done, use a fork to scrape the flesh into spaghetti strands.
7. Toss the spaghetti squash with pesto sauce and halved cherry tomatoes.
8. Garnish with fresh basil leaves and grated Parmesan cheese if desired.
9. Serve your delightful Spaghetti Squash with Pesto and Cherry Tomatoes.

Stuffed Peppadew Peppers with Cream Cheese

Prep Time: 15 minutes / Cook Time: 10 minutes
Servings: 4 servings / Mode: Air Fry

Ingredients:

- 16-20 Peppadew peppers

- 120g cream cheese
- 60g feta cheese, crumbled
- 2 cloves garlic, minced
- Fresh basil leaves (for garnish)
- Salt and pepper to taste

Preparation Instructions:

1. Preheat your dual zone air fryer to 375°F using the Air Fry mode.
2. In a mixing bowl, combine cream cheese, crumbled feta cheese, minced garlic, salt, and pepper. Mix until well combined.
3. Carefully fill each Peppadew pepper with the cream cheese mixture.
4. Place the stuffed peppers in the air fryer basket and cook for about 8-10 minutes, or until the peppers are heated through and slightly blistered.
5. Garnish with fresh basil leaves and serve your delicious Stuffed Peppadew Peppers with Cream Cheese.

Coconut-Crusted Tofu with Mango Salsa

Prep Time: 15 minutes / Cook Time: 15 minutes
Servings: 4 / Mode: Air Fry

Ingredients:

- 400g firm tofu, cut into cubes
- 60g shredded coconut
- 30g panko breadcrumbs
- 1 egg, beaten
- 30ml coconut milk
- Salt and pepper to taste
- Cooking spray
- Mango salsa (store-bought or homemade, for serving)

Preparation Instructions:

1. Preheat your dual zone air fryer to 375°F using the Air Fry mode.
2. In a shallow dish, combine shredded coconut and panko breadcrumbs. Season with salt and pepper.
3. In another bowl, mix together beaten egg and coconut milk.
4. Dip each tofu cube into the egg mixture and then roll it in the coconut breadcrumb mixture, pressing gently to adhere.
5. Place the coated tofu cubes in the air fryer basket. Spray them with cooking spray to help with browning.
6. Air fry for about 12-15 minutes, flipping halfway through, or until the tofu is golden brown and crispy.
7. Serve the Coconut-Crusted Tofu with Mango Salsa for a delightful meal.

Stuffed Bell Peppers with Brown Rice and Lentils

Prep Time: 20 minutes / Cook Time: 40 minutes
Servings: 4 / Mode: Bake

Ingredients:

- 4 large bell peppers, any colour
- 120g brown rice, cooked
- 120g green or brown lentils, cooked
- 1 can (15 oz) diced tomatoes
- 1 small onion, finely chopped
- 2 cloves garlic, minced
- 30g grated Parmesan cheese
- Fresh parsley (for garnish)
- Salt and pepper to taste

Preparation Instructions:

1. Preheat your dual zone air fryer to 375°F using the Bake mode.
2. Cut the tops off the bell peppers and remove the seeds and membranes. Set aside.
3. In a skillet, heat a little oil over medium heat. Add finely chopped onion and minced garlic. Sauté for about 3-4 minutes until softened.
4. Stir in the cooked brown rice, cooked lentils, diced tomatoes, grated Parmesan cheese, salt, and pepper. Cook for an additional 3-4 minutes until heated through.
5. Carefully stuff each bell pepper with the rice and lentil mixture.
6. Place the stuffed bell peppers in the air fryer basket and bake for about 30-35 minutes, or until the peppers are tender and slightly charred.
7. Garnish with fresh parsley and serve your delicious Stuffed Bell Peppers with Brown Rice and Lentils.

Veggie Pakoras

Prep Time: 20 minutes / Cook Time: 10 minutes
Servings: 4 / Mode: Max Crisp

Ingredients:

- 120g chickpea flour
- 1 tsp garam masala
- 1/2 tsp cumin
- 1/2 tsp Chilli powder
- Salt to taste
- 120ml water
- 1 small onion, thinly sliced
- 1 small potato, thinly sliced
- 1 small zucchini, thinly sliced
- Vegetable oil for frying

Preparation Instructions:

1. Preheat your dual zone air fryer to the Max Crisp mode.
2. In a mixing bowl, combine chickpea flour, garam masala, cumin, Chilli powder, and salt.
3. Gradually add water and whisk until you have a smooth batter.
4. Dip the thinly sliced vegetables into the batter to coat them.
5. Place the coated vegetables in the air fryer basket. Cook in batches for about 8-10 minutes or until they are crispy and golden brown.
6. Remove and drain on paper towels.
7. Serve your delicious Veggie Pakoras with chutney or dipping sauce of your choice.

Spicy Potato Wedges with Herbed Yogurt Dip

Prep Time: 15 minutes / Cook Time: 20 minutes
Servings: 4 / Mode: Air Fry

Ingredients:

- 4 large potatoes, cut into wedges
- 30ml olive oil
- 2 tsp paprika
- 1 tsp chilli powder
- Salt and pepper to taste
- 240ml Greek yoghourt
- 2 tbsp chopped fresh herbs (e.g., parsley, dill, mint)
- 1 clove garlic, minced
- Juice of 1 lemon

Preparation Instructions:

1. Preheat your dual zone air fryer to 375°F using the Air Fry mode.
2. In a large mixing bowl, combine potato wedges, olive oil, paprika, chilli powder, salt, and pepper. Toss to coat evenly.
3. Place the potato wedges in the air fryer basket. Cook for about 18-20 minutes, shaking the basket halfway through, or until the wedges are crispy and golden brown.
4. While the wedges are cooking, prepare the herbed yogurt dip. In a bowl, mix Greek yogurt, chopped fresh herbs, minced garlic, and lemon juice. Season with salt and pepper to taste.
5. Serve the Spicy Potato Wedges with the Herbed Yogurt Dip.

Smoky Baba Ganoush-Stuffed Bell Peppers

Prep Time: 20 minutes / Cook Time: 30 minutes
Servings: 4 / Mode: Roast

Ingredients:

- 4 large bell peppers, any colour
- 2 large eggplants
- 2 cloves garlic, minced
- Juice of 1 lemon
- 30ml tahini
- 30ml olive oil
- 1 tsp smoked paprika
- Salt and pepper to taste
- Fresh parsley leaves (for garnish)

Preparation Instructions:

1. Preheat your dual zone air fryer to 375°F using the Roast mode.
2. Cut the tops off the bell peppers and remove the seeds and membranes. Set aside.
3. Pierce the eggplants with a fork in several places. Place them in the air fryer basket. Roast for about 25-30 minutes or until the eggplants are tender and the skin is charred.
4. Remove the eggplants from the air fryer and let them cool. Once cool, peel the skin and scoop out the flesh into a bowl.
5. Add minced garlic, lemon juice, tahini, olive oil, smoked paprika, salt, and pepper to the eggplant flesh. Mash and mix everything together until you have a smooth baba ganoush mixture.
6. Stuff each bell pepper with the baba ganoush mixture.
7. Place the stuffed bell peppers in the air fryer basket and roast for another 10-12 minutes until they are heated through.
8. Garnish with fresh parsley leaves and serve your delightful Smoky Baba Ganoush-Stuffed Bell Peppers.

Stuffed Acorn Squash with Wild Rice and Cranberries

Prep Time: 20 minutes / Cook Time: 50 minutes
Servings: 4 / Mode: Bake

Ingredients:

- 2 acorn squash, halved and seeds removed
- 240g wild rice, cooked
- 60g dried cranberries
- 60g pecans, chopped
- 1 small onion, finely chopped
- 2 cloves garlic, minced
- 30ml olive oil
- 1 tsp dried thyme
- Salt and pepper to taste
- Fresh parsley (for garnish)

Preparation Instructions:

1. Preheat your dual zone air fryer to 375°F using the Bake mode.
2. Rub the inside of each acorn squash half with olive oil and season with salt and pepper. Place them in the air fryer basket.
3. Bake for about 35-40 minutes or until the squash is tender.
4. While the squash is baking, prepare the stuffing. In a skillet, heat olive oil over medium heat. Add chopped onion and minced garlic. Sauté for about 3-4 minutes until softened.
5. Stir in cooked wild rice, dried cranberries, chopped pecans, dried thyme, salt, and pepper. Cook for an additional 5 minutes to heat everything through.
6. Once the squash is done, stuff each squash half with the wild rice and cranberry mixture.
7. Return the stuffed squash halves to the air fryer and bake for an additional 10-12 minutes until everything is heated through.
8. Garnish with fresh parsley and serve your delicious Stuffed Acorn Squash with Wild Rice and Cranberries.

Stuffed Portobello Mushrooms with Spinach and Goat Cheese

Prep Time: 15 minutes / Cook Time: 15 minutes
Servings: 4 / Mode: Max Crisp

Ingredients:

- 4 large portobello mushrooms, stems removed
- 240g fresh spinach
- 100g goat cheese, crumbled
- 2 cloves garlic, minced
- 30ml olive oil
- Salt and pepper to taste
- Fresh basil leaves (for garnish)

Preparation Instructions:

1. Preheat your dual zone air fryer to the Max Crisp mode.
2. In a skillet, heat olive oil over medium heat. Add minced garlic and cook for about 1 minute until fragrant.
3. Add fresh spinach to the skillet and sauté until wilted, about 3-4 minutes. Season with salt and pepper.
4. Place the portobello mushrooms in the air fryer basket and fill them with the sautéed spinach and crumbled goat cheese.
5. Air fry for about 12-15 minutes until the mushrooms are tender and the cheese is slightly browned.
6. Garnish with fresh basil leaves and serve your

delightful Stuffed Portobello Mushrooms with Spinach and Goat Cheese.

Sweet Potato and Chickpea Cakes

Prep Time: 20 minutes / Cook Time: 20 minutes
Servings: 4 / Mode: Air Fry

Ingredients:

- 2 medium sweet potatoes, peeled and grated
- 400g canned chickpeas, drained and mashed
- 1 small onion, finely chopped
- 2 cloves garlic, minced
- 30g breadcrumbs
- 1 tsp ground cumin
- 1/2 tsp smoked paprika
- Salt and pepper to taste
- Cooking spray

Preparation Instructions:

1. Preheat your dual zone air fryer to 375°F using the Air Fry mode.
2. In a mixing bowl, combine grated sweet potatoes, mashed chickpeas, chopped onion, minced garlic, breadcrumbs, ground cumin, smoked paprika, salt, and pepper.
3. Form the mixture into patties.
4. Place the sweet potato and chickpea cakes in the air fryer basket. Spray them with cooking spray.
5. Air fry for about 18-20 minutes, flipping halfway through, or until the cakes are golden brown and crispy.
6. Serve your Sweet Potato and Chickpea Cakes with your favourite dipping sauce.

Smoky Eggplant Dip (Baba Ganoush)

Prep Time: 15 minutes / Cook Time: 30 minutes
Servings: 6 / Mode: Roast

Ingredients:

- 2 large eggplants
- 2 cloves garlic, minced
- Juice of 1 lemon
- 60ml tahini
- 30ml olive oil, plus extra for garnish
- 1 tsp smoked paprika
- Salt and pepper to taste
- Fresh parsley leaves (for garnish)
- Pita bread or veggies (for serving)

Preparation Instructions:

1. Preheat your dual zone air fryer to 375°F using the Roast mode.

2. Pierce the eggplants with a fork in several places. Place them in the air fryer basket. Roast for about 25-30 minutes or until the eggplants are tender and the skin is charred.
3. Remove the eggplants from the air fryer and let them cool. Once cool, peel the skin and scoop out the flesh into a bowl.
4. Add minced garlic, lemon juice, tahini, olive oil, smoked paprika, salt, and pepper to the eggplant flesh. Mash and mix everything together until you have a smooth baba ganoush.
5. Drizzle with extra olive oil and garnish with fresh parsley leaves.
6. Serve your Smoky Eggplant Dip with pita bread or veggies for dipping.

Polenta Fries with Marinara Dipping Sauce

Prep Time: 15 minutes / Cook Time: 15 minutes
Servings: 4 / Mode: Air Fry

Ingredients:

- 240g instant polenta
- 1200ml water
- Salt and pepper to taste
- Cooking spray
- 240ml marinara sauce (store-bought or homemade)

Preparation Instructions:

1. Preheat your dual zone air fryer to 375°F using the Air Fry mode.
2. In a saucepan, bring 120ml of water to a boil. Gradually whisk in the instant polenta. Reduce heat to low and cook for about 5 minutes, stirring constantly until the polenta is thick and smooth.
3. Season with salt and pepper to taste.
4. Pour the polenta onto a greased baking sheet and spread it evenly to about 1/2-inch thickness. Let it cool and set for about 10 minutes.
5. Cut the polenta into fries or wedges.
6. Place the polenta fries in the air fryer basket and spray them with cooking spray.
7. Air fry for about 12-15 minutes until the fries are crispy and golden brown.
8. Serve the Polenta Fries with marinara sauce for dipping.

Okra Fritters with Tamarind Chutney

Prep Time: 20 minutes / Cook Time: 15 minutes
Servings: 4 / Mode: Max Crisp

Ingredients:

- 240g fresh okra, thinly sliced
- 1 small onion, finely chopped
- 2 cloves garlic, minced
- 1 green Chilli pepper, minced (adjust to taste)
- 60g chickpea flour (besan)
- 1 tsp ground cumin
- 1/2 tsp ground coriander
- 1/2 tsp Chilli powder
- Salt to taste
- Cooking oil for frying
- Tamarind chutney (store-bought or homemade, for dipping)

Preparation Instructions:

1. Preheat your dual zone air fryer to the Max Crisp mode.
2. In a mixing bowl, combine sliced okra, chopped onion, minced garlic, minced green Chilli pepper, chickpea flour, ground cumin, ground coriander, Chilli powder, and salt. Mix well to coat the okra evenly.
3. Form the mixture into small fritters.
4. Place the okra fritters in the air fryer basket. Cook for about 10-12 minutes or until they are crispy and golden brown.
5. Remove and drain on paper towels.
6. Serve the Okra Fritters with tamarind chutney for dipping.

Polenta Fries with Marinara Dipping Sauce

Prep Time: 15 minutes / Cook Time: 15 minutes
Servings: 4 / Mode: Air Fry

Ingredients:

- 240g instant polenta
- 1200ml water
- Salt and pepper to taste
- Cooking spray
- 240ml marinara sauce (store-bought or homemade)

Preparation Instructions:

1. Preheat your dual zone air fryer to 375°F using the Air Fry mode.
2. In a saucepan, bring 1200ml of water to a boil. Gradually whisk in the instant polenta. Reduce heat to low and cook for about 5 minutes, stirring constantly until the polenta is thick and smooth.
3. Season with salt and pepper to taste.
4. Pour the polenta onto a greased baking sheet and spread it evenly to about 1/2-inch thickness. Let it cool and set for about 10 minutes.
5. Cut the polenta into fries or wedges.

6. Place the polenta fries in the air fryer basket and spray them with cooking spray.
7. Air fry for about 12-15 minutes until the fries are crispy and golden brown.
8. Serve the Polenta Fries with marinara sauce for dipping.

Sweet Potato Gnocchi with Sage Butter

Prep Time: 30 minutes / Cook Time: 15 minutes
Servings: 4 / Mode: Air Fry

Ingredients:

- For the Gnocchi:
- 2 large sweet potatoes (about 700g), peeled and cubed
- 240g all-purpose flour
- 1 tsp salt
- 1/2 tsp nutmeg
- For the Sage Butter Sauce:
- 60g unsalted butter
- 8-10 fresh sage leaves
- Salt and pepper to taste
- Grated Parmesan cheese (optional, for serving)

Preparation Instructions:

1. Preheat your dual zone air fryer to 375°F using the Air Fry mode.
2. Boil the sweet potato cubes until tender, about 10-12 minutes. Drain and let them cool slightly.
3. Mash the cooked sweet potatoes or pass them through a ricer.
4. In a large bowl, combine the mashed sweet potatoes, all-purpose flour, salt, and nutmeg. Knead the mixture until it forms a soft dough.
5. Divide the dough into small portions and roll each portion into a long rope about 1-inch thick. Cut the ropes into bite-sized pieces to form gnocchi.
6. Place the gnocchi in the air fryer basket and air fry for about 8-10 minutes until they are golden brown and crispy.
7. While the gnocchi are air frying, prepare the sage butter sauce. In a skillet, melt the butter over medium heat. Add fresh sage leaves and cook until they become crispy, about 2-3 minutes. Season with salt and pepper.
8. Toss the cooked gnocchi in the sage butter sauce.
9. Serve your Sweet Potato Gnocchi with Sage Butter with optional grated Parmesan cheese on top.

Vegan Samosas

Prep Time: 30 minutes / Cook Time: 20 minutes
Servings: 12 samosas / Mode: Air Fry

Ingredients:

- For the Filling:
- 2 medium potatoes, boiled and diced
- 100g green peas, boiled
- 1 small onion, finely chopped
- 2 cloves garlic, minced
- 1 tsp cumin seeds
- 1 tsp ground coriander
- 1/2 tsp turmeric powder
- 1/2 tsp Chilli powder (adjust to taste)
- Salt to taste
- Cooking oil for sautéing
- For the Samosa Wrappers:
- 12 samosa wrappers (store-bought or homemade)

Preparation Instructions:

1. Preheat your dual zone air fryer to 375°F using the Air Fry mode.
2. In a skillet, heat some cooking oil over medium heat. Add cumin seeds and let them sizzle for a few seconds.
3. Add chopped onion and minced garlic. Sauté until the onion is translucent.
4. Stir in diced boiled potatoes, boiled green peas, ground coriander, turmeric powder, chilli powder, and salt. Cook for another 3-4 minutes to combine the flavours. Remove from heat and let the filling cool.
5. Take a samosa wrapper and place it on a clean surface. Fold it into a triangle, sealing the edges with a bit of water.
6. Fill each samosa wrapper with the cooled potato and pea mixture.
7. Place the samosas in the air fryer basket and air fry for about 15-20 minutes, flipping halfway through, or until they are crispy and golden brown.
8. Serve your Vegan Samosas hot with your favourite dipping sauce.

Parsnip and Sage Ravioli

Prep Time: 30 minutes / Cook Time: 10 minutes
Servings: 4 / Mode: Air Fry

Ingredients:

- For the Ravioli:
- 250g fresh parsnip and sage ravioli
- Salt and black pepper to taste
- For the Sage Butter Sauce:
- 60g unsalted butter
- 8-10 fresh sage leaves
- Grated Parmesan cheese (optional, for serving)

Preparation Instructions:

1. Boil the fresh parsnip and sage ravioli according to the package instructions until they are al dente.

Drain and set aside.

2. Preheat your dual zone air fryer to 375°F using the Air Fry mode.
3. Place the cooked ravioli in the air fryer basket and air fry for about 4-5 minutes until they become crispy and golden.
4. While the ravioli are air frying, prepare the sage butter sauce. In a skillet, melt the butter over medium heat. Add fresh sage leaves and cook until they become crispy, about 2-3 minutes. Season with salt and black pepper.
5. Toss the air-fried ravioli in the sage butter sauce.
6. Serve your Parsnip and Sage Ravioli with optional grated Parmesan cheese on top.

Brussels Sprouts with Pomegranate Molasses

Prep Time 10 minutes / Cook Time: 15 minutes
Servings: 4 / Mode: Roast

Ingredients:

- 500g Brussels sprouts, trimmed and halved
- 30ml olive oil
- 30ml pomegranate molasses
- Salt and black pepper to taste
- Pomegranate seeds (for garnish, optional)

Preparation Instructions:

1. Preheat your dual zone air fryer to 375°F using the Roast mode.
2. In a large bowl, toss the trimmed and halved Brussels sprouts with olive oil, pomegranate molasses, salt, and black pepper until well coated.
3. Place the Brussels sprouts in the air fryer basket and roast for about 12-15 minutes, shaking the basket halfway through, or until they are tender and slightly caramelised.
4. Garnish with pomegranate seeds if desired and serve your Brussels Sprouts with Pomegranate Molasses.

Butternut Squash and Kale Salad with Tahini Dressing

Prep Time: 20 minutes / Cook Time: 20 minutes
Servings: 4 / Mode: Roast

Ingredients:

- For the Salad:
- 500g butternut squash, peeled and cubed
- 200g kale leaves, stemmed and torn into bite-sized pieces
- 30ml olive oil
- Salt and black pepper to taste
- For the Tahini Dressing:
- 60ml tahini
- 30ml lemon juice
- 1 clove garlic, minced
- 30ml water
- Salt and black pepper to taste

Preparation Instructions:

1. Preheat your dual zone air fryer to 375°F using the Roast mode.
2. In a large bowl, toss the cubed butternut squash with olive oil, salt, and black pepper until well coated.
3. Place the butternut squash in one zone of the air fryer and roast for about 18-20 minutes, shaking the basket halfway through, or until the squash is tender and slightly caramelised.
4. In the other zone, place the torn kale leaves and roast for about 3-5 minutes until they become crispy.
5. While the vegetables are roasting, prepare the tahini dressing by whisking together tahini, lemon juice, minced garlic, water, salt, and black pepper in a bowl.
6. Once the vegetables are done, assemble the salad by placing the roasted butternut squash and kale in a serving dish. Drizzle with the tahini dressing.
7. Serve your Butternut Squash and Kale Salad with Tahini Dressing.

Cumin-Spiced Carrot Fries

Prep Time: 10 minutes / Cook Time: 15 minutes
Servings: 4 / Mode: Air Fry

Ingredients:

- 500g carrots, peeled and cut into fries
- 30ml olive oil
- 5g ground cumin
- 5g ground coriander
- Salt and black pepper to taste

Preparation Instructions:

1. Preheat your dual zone air fryer to 375°F using the Air Fry mode.
2. In a large bowl, toss the carrot fries with olive oil, ground cumin, ground coriander, salt, and black pepper until well coated.
3. Place the carrot fries in the air fryer basket and air fry for about 12-15 minutes until they are crispy and golden brown.
4. Serve your Cumin-Spiced Carrot Fries hot.

Chapter 6 Sides and Appetisers

Devils on Horseback

Prep Time: 15 minutes / Cook Time: 10 minutes
Servings: 4 / Mode: Max Crisp

Ingredients:
- 12 large prunes or dates
- 12 whole almonds or pieces of blue cheese
- 6 slices of bacon, cut in half
- Toothpicks, for securing

Preparation Instructions:
1. If using prunes, make a small slit in each prune and remove the pit. If using dates, carefully make a lengthwise cut in each date and remove the pit. Stuff each prune or date with an almond or a small piece of blue cheese.
2. Take a half-slice of bacon and wrap it around each stuffed prune or date, securing it with a toothpick. Repeat for all.
3. Preheat your dual zone air fryer to 375°F.
4. Place the bacon-wrapped prunes or dates in a single layer in one zone of your dual zone air fryer. Make sure they are not touching each other even when cooking.
5. Set one zone of your air fryer to Max Crisp mode at 375°F and cook for about 5 minutes, or until the bacon is crispy.
6. Remove the Devils on Horseback from the air fryer and let them cool slightly. Transfer to a serving platter and serve while they're still warm.

Chilli and Lime Edamame

Prep Time: 5 minutes / Cook Time: 5 minutes
Servings: 4 / Mode: Air Fry

Ingredients:
- 400g frozen edamame pods, thawed
- 15ml olive oil
- 1-2 red chillies, finely chopped
- Zest and juice of 1 lime
- Salt to taste

Preparation Instructions:
1. Preheat your dual zone air fryer to 350°F using the Steam mode.
2. Place the thawed edamame pods in one zone and steam for about 4-5 minutes or until they are tender.
3. In a bowl, toss the steamed edamame with olive oil, finely chopped red chillies, lime zest, lime juice, and salt until well coated.

4. Transfer the seasoned edamame to the other zone of the air fryer preheated to 375°F using the Air Fry mode.
5. Air fry for an additional 4-5 minutes, shaking the basket halfway through, until the edamame become slightly crispy.
6. Serve your Chilli and Lime Edamame hot.

Camembert-Stuffed Phyllo Parcels

Prep Time: 15 minutes / Cook Time: 10 minutes
Servings: 4 / Mode: Bake

Ingredients:
- 4 sheets of phyllo pastry
- 4 small Camembert cheese rounds
- 30ml melted butter
- Honey (for drizzling, optional)
- Fresh rosemary sprigs (for garnish, optional)

Preparation Instructions:
1. Preheat your dual zone air fryer to 375°F using the Bake mode.
2. Take one sheet of phyllo pastry and brush it with melted butter. Place another sheet on top and repeat until you have a stack of 4 sheets.
3. Place a small Camembert cheese round in the centre of each phyllo stack.
4. Carefully fold the phyllo pastry over the Camembert to create a parcel. Brush the top with more melted butter.
5. Place the Camembert-Stuffed Phyllo Parcels in one zone of the air fryer and bake for about 8-10 minutes until the phyllo is golden brown and the cheese is melted.
6. Optionally, drizzle with honey and garnish with fresh rosemary sprigs.
7. Serve your Camembert-Stuffed Phyllo Parcels hot, accompanied by your choice of crackers or bread.

Stuffed Mini Bell Peppers with Couscous and Mint

Prep Time: 20 minutes / Cook Time: 15 minutes
Servings: 4 / Mode: Bake

Ingredients:
- 12 mini bell peppers, halved and seeds removed
- 150g couscous
- 300ml vegetable broth

- 30ml olive oil
- 15g fresh mint leaves, chopped
- 30g feta cheese, crumbled
- Salt and black pepper to taste

Preparation Instructions:

1. Preheat your dual zone air fryer to 375°F using the Bake mode.
2. In a heatproof bowl, combine the couscous and vegetable broth. Cover and let it sit for 5 minutes, then fluff with a fork.
3. In a separate bowl, mix the cooked couscous, olive oil, chopped mint, crumbled feta cheese, salt, and black pepper.
4. Stuff the mini bell pepper halves with the couscous mixture.
5. Place the stuffed mini bell peppers in one zone of the air fryer and bake for about 12-15 minutes until the peppers are tender and slightly charred.
6. Serve your Stuffed Mini Bell Peppers with Couscous and Mint as a delightful appetiser or side dish.

Stuffed Mini Pumpkins with Wild Rice and Cranberries

Prep Time: 20 minutes / Cook Time: 30 minutes
Servings: 4 servings / Mode: Roast

Ingredients:

- 4 mini pumpkins, tops removed and seeds scooped out
- 200g wild rice, cooked
- 60g dried cranberries
- 30g toasted pecans, chopped
- 15g fresh parsley, chopped
- 30ml olive oil
- Salt and black pepper to taste

Preparation Instructions:

1. Preheat one zone of your dual zone air fryer to 375°F using the Roast mode.
2. In a bowl, combine the cooked wild rice, dried cranberries, toasted pecans, chopped parsley, olive oil, salt, and black pepper.
3. Stuff each mini pumpkin with the wild rice mixture.
4. Place the stuffed mini pumpkins in the preheated air fryer and roast for about 25-30 minutes until the pumpkins are tender and the filling is heated through.
5. Serve your Stuffed Mini Pumpkins with Wild Rice and Cranberries as a delightful autumn dish.

Beetroot and Goat Cheese Crostinis

Prep Time: 15 minutes / Cook Time: 10 minutes
Servings: 4 servings / Mode: Air Fry

Ingredients:

- 4 slices of baguette
- 100g goat cheese
- 2 medium beetroot, cooked and sliced
- Fresh thyme leaves (for garnish)
- 15ml honey (for drizzling, optional)
- Olive oil (for brushing)
- Salt and black pepper to taste

Preparation Instructions:

1. Preheat your dual zone air fryer to 375°F using the Air Fry mode.
2. Brush the baguette slices with olive oil and air fry them for about 3-5 minutes until they are crispy and golden brown.
3. Spread goat cheese on each baguette slice.
4. Top with cooked beetroot slices.
5. Season with salt and black pepper.
6. Optionally, drizzle with honey and garnish with fresh thyme leaves.
7. Serve your Beetroot and Goat Cheese Crostinis as a tasty appetiser or snack.

Stuffed Bell Peppers with Bulgur and Raisins

Prep Time: 20 minutes / Cook Time: 40 minutes
Servings: 4 / Mode: Bake

Ingredients:

- 4 bell peppers, any colour, tops removed and seeds removed
- 150g bulgur, cooked
- 60g raisins
- 30g pine nuts, toasted
- 1 small onion, finely chopped
- 15ml olive oil
- 5g ground cinnamon
- Salt and black pepper to taste
- Fresh parsley leaves (for garnish)

Preparation Instructions:

1. Preheat one zone of your dual zone air fryer to 375°F using the Bake mode.
2. In a skillet, heat olive oil over medium heat. Add the chopped onion and sauté until translucent.
3. Add the cooked bulgur, raisins, toasted pine nuts, ground cinnamon, salt, and black pepper to the skillet. Stir well to combine.
4. Stuff each bell pepper with the bulgur and raisin mixture.
5. Place the stuffed bell peppers in the preheated air fryer zone and bake for about 35-40 minutes until the peppers are tender and slightly charred.
6. Garnish with fresh parsley leaves and serve your

Stuffed Bell Peppers with Bulgur and Raisins as a delicious and nutritious dish.

Pigs in a Blanket with Mustard Dip

Prep Time: 15 minutes / Cook Time: 10 minutes
Servings: 4 / Mode: Air Fry

Ingredients:

- 8 cocktail sausages
- 1 sheet of puff pastry
- 30ml Dijon mustard
- 30ml honey (for dipping)
- Sesame seeds (for garnish, optional)

Preparation Instructions:

1. Preheat your dual zone air fryer to 375°F using the Air Fry mode.
2. Cut the puff pastry sheet into thin strips.
3. Wrap each cocktail sausage with a strip of puff pastry.
4. Place the wrapped sausages in one zone of the air fryer and air fry for about 8-10 minutes until the pastry is golden brown and the sausages are heated through.
5. In a small bowl, mix Dijon mustard and honey for the dipping sauce.
6. Optionally, garnish with sesame seeds.
7. Serve your Pigs in a Blanket with Mustard Dip as a tasty party snack or appetiser.

Panko-Crusted Deviled Eggs

Prep Time: 20 minutes / Cook Time: 10 minutes
Servings: 4 / Mode: Bake

Ingredients:

- 4 hard-boiled eggs, peeled and halved
- 60g mayonnaise
- 15g Dijon mustard
- 15g sweet relish
- Salt and black pepper to taste
- 30g panko breadcrumbs
- Fresh chives (for garnish)

Preparation Instructions:

1. Preheat one zone of your dual zone air fryer to 375°F using the Bake mode.
2. Carefully remove the yolks from the hard-boiled egg halves and place them in a bowl.
3. Mash the egg yolks and mix in mayonnaise, Dijon mustard, sweet relish, salt, and black pepper to create a deviled egg filling.
4. Fill each egg white half with the deviled egg filling.
5. Roll the filled egg halves in panko breadcrumbs to coat.
6. Place the panko-crusted deviled eggs in the preheated air fryer zone and bake for about 8-10 minutes until the breadcrumbs are golden brown.

7. Garnish with fresh chives.
8. Serve your Panko-Crusted Deviled Eggs crunchy.

Sweet Potato Tots with Maple Mustard Dip

Prep Time: 20 minutes / Cook Time: 15 minutes
Servings: 4 / Mode: Air Fry

Ingredients:

- 2 large sweet potatoes, peeled and grated
- 60g breadcrumbs
- 30ml olive oil
- 5g paprika
- Salt and black pepper to taste
- For the Maple Mustard Dip:
- 30ml maple syrup
- 15ml Dijon mustard
- 5ml apple cider vinegar

Preparation Instructions:

1. Preheat your dual zone air fryer to 375°F using the Air Fry mode.
2. In a bowl, combine the grated sweet potatoes, breadcrumbs, olive oil, paprika, salt, and black pepper. Mix well.
3. Shape the mixture into tots or small cylindrical shapes.
4. Place the sweet potato tots in one zone of the air fryer and air fry for about 12-15 minutes until they are crispy and golden brown.
5. While the tots are cooking, prepare the Maple Mustard Dip by whisking together maple syrup, Dijon mustard, and apple cider vinegar in a small bowl.
6. Serve the Sweet Potato Tots with the Maple Mustard Dip for a delightful and slightly sweet snack.

Pesto and Sun-Dried Tomato Arancini

Prep Time: 30 minutes / Cook Time: 15 minutes
Servings: 4 / Mode: Air Fry

Ingredients:

- 200g Arborio rice
- 500ml vegetable broth
- 30ml olive oil
- 30g Parmesan cheese, grated
- 60g pesto sauce
- 60g sun-dried tomatoes, chopped
- Salt and black pepper to taste
- 2 large eggs, beaten
- 60g breadcrumbs

Preparation Instructions:

1. Preheat one zone of your dual zone air fryer to

375°F using the Air Fry mode.

2. In a saucepan, bring the vegetable broth to a simmer and keep it warm.

3. In another pan, heat olive oil over medium heat. Add Arborio rice and cook for a few minutes until translucent.

4. Gradually add warm vegetable broth to the rice, one ladle at a time, stirring constantly until the liquid is absorbed and the rice is creamy and cooked.

5. Remove the cooked rice from heat and let it cool slightly. Stir in grated Parmesan cheese, pesto sauce, chopped sun-dried tomatoes, salt, and black pepper.

6. Take small portions of the mixture and shape them into balls.

7. Dip each arancini ball in beaten eggs and then roll in breadcrumbs to coat.

8. Place the arancini balls in the preheated air fryer zone and air fry for about 10-15 minutes until they are crispy and golden brown.

9. Serve the Pesto and Sun-Dried Tomato Arancini as a delicious Italian-inspired appetiser.

Blackberry-Glazed Duck Bites

Prep Time: 15 minutes / Cook Time: 20 minutes
Servings: 4 / Mode: Roast

Ingredients:
- 200g duck breast, thinly sliced
- 100g blackberries
- 30ml balsamic vinegar
- 30g brown sugar
- Salt and black pepper to taste

Preparation Instructions:
1. Preheat one zone of your dual zone air fryer to 375°F using the Roast mode.

2. In a saucepan, combine blackberries, balsamic vinegar, and brown sugar. Cook over medium heat until the mixture thickens and the blackberries break down to form a glaze. Season with salt and black pepper.

3. Thread the thinly sliced duck breast onto skewers.

4. Place the duck skewers in the preheated air fryer zone and roast for about 15-20 minutes until the duck is cooked and slightly crispy.

5. Brush the roasted duck skewers with the blackberry glaze.

6. Serve your Blackberry-Glazed Duck Bites as a flavorful and elegant appetiser.

Cheddar and Chive Potato Skins

Prep Time: 15 minutes / Cook Time: 25 minutes
Servings: 4 / Mode: Bake

Ingredients:
- 4 large russet potatoes
- 150g cheddar cheese, grated
- 30g fresh chives, chopped
- 30ml olive oil
- Salt and black pepper to taste
- Sour cream (for serving)

Preparation Instructions:
1. Preheat one zone of your dual zone air fryer to 375°F using the Bake mode.

2. Scrub and wash the potatoes thoroughly. Pierce each potato with a fork a few times.

3. Place the potatoes in the preheated air fryer zone and bake for about 45-50 minutes until they are tender.

4. Remove the potatoes from the air fryer and let them cool slightly.

5. Cut the potatoes in half lengthwise and scoop out the flesh, leaving a thin layer attached to the skins.

6. Brush the potato skins with olive oil and season with salt and black pepper.

7. Return the potato skins to the air fryer and bake for an additional 10-15 minutes until they become crispy.

8. Remove the potato skins from the air fryer and sprinkle grated cheddar cheese over each one. Place them back in the air fryer for a few minutes until the cheese is melted and bubbly.

9. Garnish with chopped fresh chives and serve with sour cream on the side for dipping.

Spinach and Feta-Stuffed Phyllo Triangles

Prep Time: 20 minutes / Cook Time: 15 minutes
Servings: 4 / Mode: Air Fry

Ingredients:
- 200g fresh spinach leaves
- 150g feta cheese, crumbled
- 4 sheets of phyllo pastry
- 30ml olive oil
- Salt and black pepper to taste

Preparation Instructions:
1. Preheat one zone of your dual zone air fryer to 375°F using the Air Fry mode.

2. In a skillet, wilt the fresh spinach over medium heat. Remove excess moisture by pressing the spinach between paper towels. Chop the spinach finely.

3. In a bowl, combine the chopped spinach and crumbled feta cheese. Season with salt and black pepper.

4. Take one sheet of phyllo pastry and brush it with olive oil. Place another sheet on top and brush with olive oil. Repeat this process with the remaining

two sheets.

5. Cut the layered phyllo pastry into squares or rectangles.
6. Place a spoonful of the spinach and feta mixture on each piece of phyllo pastry.
7. Fold the phyllo pastry over the filling to create triangles or rectangles.
8. Place the stuffed phyllo triangles in the preheated air fryer zone and air fry for about 10-15 minutes until they are golden brown and crispy.
9. Serve the Spinach and Feta-Stuffed Phyllo Triangles as a delightful appetiser or snack.

Battered Pickled Onions

Prep Time: 15 minutes / Cook Time: 10 minutes
Servings: 4 / Mode: Max Crisp

Ingredients:
- 200g pickled onions
- 100g all-purpose flour
- 2 large eggs, beaten
- 60ml milk
- Salt and black pepper to taste
- Cooking spray (for greasing)

Preparation Instructions:
1. Preheat one zone of your dual zone air fryer to the Max Crisp mode.
2. In a bowl, whisk together the all-purpose flour, beaten eggs, milk, salt, and black pepper to create a smooth batter.
3. Dip each pickled onion into the batter, ensuring it is well coated.
4. Place the battered pickled onions in the preheated air fryer zone and cook for about 8-10 minutes until they are crispy and golden brown.
5. Remove the battered pickled onions from the air fryer and let them cool slightly before serving.

Caramelised Onion and Fig Flatbreads

Prep Time: 15 minutes / Cook Time: 15 minutes
Servings: 4 / Mode: Bake

Ingredients:
- 2 flatbreads
- 2 large onions, thinly sliced
- 4 dried figs, thinly sliced
- 30ml olive oil
- 30g goat cheese, crumbled
- Fresh thyme leaves (for garnish)
- Salt and black pepper to taste

Preparation Instructions:
1. Preheat one zone of your dual zone air fryer to 375°F using the Bake mode.

2. In a skillet, heat olive oil over medium-low heat. Add the thinly sliced onions and cook, stirring occasionally, for about 10-15 minutes until they are caramelised and golden brown. Season with salt and black pepper.
3. Place the flatbreads on a baking sheet and brush them with olive oil.
4. Spread the caramelised onions evenly over the flatbreads.
5. Arrange the sliced dried figs on top of the onions.
6. Sprinkle crumbled goat cheese over the figs.
7. Place the prepared flatbreads in the preheated air fryer zone and bake for about 10-12 minutes until the edges are crispy, and the cheese is melted and bubbly.
8. Garnish with fresh thyme leaves and serve your caramelised Onion and Fig Flatbreads hot.

Butternut Squash and Sage Arancini

Prep Time: 20 minutes / Cook Time: 20 minutes
Servings: 4 / Mode: Air Fry

Ingredients:
- 200g cooked butternut squash, mashed
- 200g Arborio rice, cooked and cooled
- 30g Parmesan cheese, grated
- 30g fresh sage leaves, chopped
- 2 large eggs, beaten
- Breadcrumbs (for coating)
- Cooking spray (for greasing)

Preparation Instructions:
1. Preheat one zone of your dual zone air fryer to 375°F using the Air Fry mode.
2. In a bowl, combine the mashed butternut squash, cooked Arborio rice, grated Parmesan cheese, and chopped fresh sage leaves. Mix well.
3. Shape the mixture into golf ball-sized arancini.
4. Dip each arancini ball into beaten eggs, then roll in breadcrumbs to coat evenly.
5. Place the coated arancini balls in the preheated air fryer zone and air fry for about 10-12 minutes until they are golden brown and crispy.
6. Remove the Butternut Squash and Sage Arancini from the air fryer and let them cool slightly before serving.

Polenta Fries with Roasted Garlic Aioli

Prep Time: 15 minutes / Cook Time: 15 minutes
Servings: 4 / Mode: Max Crisp

Ingredients:
- 200g cooked polenta, chilled and sliced into fries

- 30ml olive oil
- Salt and black pepper to taste
- Cooking spray (for greasing)
- For Roasted Garlic Aioli:
- 2 cloves garlic, roasted and mashed
- 150ml mayonnaise
- 15ml lemon juice
- 5ml Dijon mustard
- Salt and black pepper to taste

Preparation Instructions:

1. Preheat one zone of your dual zone air fryer to the Max Crisp mode.
2. In a bowl, toss the chilled polenta fries with olive oil, salt, and black pepper.
3. Place the seasoned polenta fries in the preheated air fryer zone and cook for about 10-12 minutes until they are crispy and golden brown.
4. While the polenta fries are cooking, prepare the Roasted Garlic Aioli. In a separate bowl, combine the roasted and mashed garlic, mayonnaise, lemon juice, Dijon mustard, salt, and black pepper. Mix until well combined.
5. Serve the Polenta Fries hot with the Roasted Garlic Aioli for dipping.

Potato and Pea Samosas

Prep Time: 30 minutes / Cook Time: 15 minutes
Servings: 4 / Mode: Max Crisp

Ingredients:

- 2 large potatoes, boiled, peeled, and diced
- 100g frozen peas, thawed
- 1 small onion, finely chopped
- 2 cloves garlic, minced
- 1 tsp cumin seeds   • 1 tsp ground coriander
- 1 tsp ground turmeric
- 1 tsp Chilli powder
- Salt and black pepper to taste
- 1 package of samosa pastry sheets
- Cooking spray (for greasing)
- Fresh cilantro leaves (for garnish)
- Tamarind chutney (for dipping)

Preparation Instructions:

1. Preheat one zone of your dual zone air fryer to the Max Crisp mode.
2. In a pan, heat some oil over medium heat. Add cumin seeds and let them sizzle for a few seconds.
3. Add the finely chopped onion and minced garlic to the pan. Sauté until the onions become translucent.
4. Stir in the diced potatoes and thawed peas. Add the ground coriander, ground turmeric, chilli powder,

salt, and black pepper. Mix well and cook for about 5 minutes until the mixture is heated through.
5. Allow the potato and pea filling to cool.
6. Take a samosa pastry sheet and cut it in half to form two triangles.
7. Place a spoonful of the potato and pea filling in the centre of each triangle.
8. Fold the pastry sheet over the filling to form a triangle shape. Seal the edges by pressing them together.
9. Spray the samosas with cooking spray.
10. Place the samosas in the preheated air fryer zone and cook for about 10-12 minutes until they are crispy and golden brown.
11. Garnish with fresh cilantro leaves and serve hot with tamarind chutney for dipping.

Saffron Risotto Balls

Prep Time: 30 minutes / Cook Time: 20 minutes
Servings: 4 / Mode: Bake

Ingredients:

- 200g Arborio rice   • 1 shallot, finely chopped
- 1 clove garlic, minced
- 1/4 tsp saffron threads
- 500ml vegetable broth
- 30g grated Parmesan cheese
- 2 large eggs   • Breadcrumbs (for coating)
- Cooking spray (for greasing)

Preparation Instructions:

1. Preheat one zone of your dual zone air fryer to 375°F using the Bake mode.
2. In a saucepan, heat the vegetable broth until it's simmering, then add the saffron threads. Let it steep for a few minutes.
3. In a separate pan, sauté the finely chopped shallot and minced garlic until translucent.
4. Add the Arborio rice to the pan and cook, stirring constantly, for a few minutes until the rice is lightly toasted.
5. Gradually add the saffron-infused vegetable broth, one ladle at a time, stirring continuously. Cook until the rice is creamy and tender.
6. Remove the risotto from heat and let it cool.
7. Once the risotto is cool, mix in the grated Parmesan cheese and beaten eggs.
8. Shape the risotto mixture into golf ball-sized balls.
9. Roll the risotto balls in breadcrumbs to coat evenly.
10. Place the coated risotto balls in the preheated air fryer zone and bake for about 15-20 minutes until they are golden brown and crispy.
11. Serve your Saffron Risotto Balls hot as a delightful appetiser or side dish.

Chapter 7 Beans, Rice & Grains

Kidney Bean and Plantain Hash

Prep Time: 15 minutes / Cook Time: 15 minutes
Servings: 2 / Mode: Roast

Ingredients:

- 1 ripe plantain, peeled and diced
- 1 can kidney beans, drained and rinsed
- 1 red bell pepper, diced
- 1 onion, chopped
- 2 cloves garlic, minced
- 1 teaspoon ground cumin
- 1 teaspoon paprika
- Salt and black pepper, to taste
- Olive oil (for cooking)
- Fresh cilantro leaves (for garnish)
- Fried or poached eggs (optional, for serving)

Preparation Instructions:

1. Preheat your dual zone air fryer to 375°F using the Roast mode.
2. In a skillet, heat a bit of olive oil over medium heat. Add chopped onions and minced garlic. Sauté until the onions are translucent.
3. Add diced plantain, red bell pepper, ground cumin, paprika, salt, and black pepper to the skillet. Cook until the plantains are golden and tender, about 5-7 minutes.
4. Stir in the kidney beans and cook for an additional 2-3 minutes until heated through.
5. Transfer the kidney bean and plantain hash to serving plates.
6. Garnish with fresh cilantro leaves.
7. Optionally, serve with fried or poached eggs for a complete meal.

Quinoa and Chickpea Salad with Lemon-Tahini Dressing

Prep Time: 15 minutes / Cook Time: 15 minutes (for quinoa)
Servings: 2 / Mode: Air Fry

Ingredients:

- 185g cooked and cooled quinoa
- 1 can chickpeas, drained and rinsed
- 1 cucumber, diced • 1 red bell pepper, diced
- Fresh parsley, chopped
- Fresh mint leaves, chopped
- Tahini • Fresh lemon juice
- Garlic, minced • Salt and black pepper, to taste

Preparation Instructions:

1. Preheat your dual zone air fryer to 350°F using the Air Fry mode.
2. Place the cooked quinoa in a bowl.
3. In a separate bowl, combine chickpeas with a drizzle of olive oil and your choice of seasonings (e.g., paprika, cumin, Chilli powder). Toss to coat.
4. Place the seasoned chickpeas in the air fryer basket using the Air Fry mode. Cook for about 10-12 minutes until they are crispy, shaking the basket occasionally.
5. In a large mixing bowl, combine the cooked quinoa, diced cucumber, diced red bell pepper, fresh parsley, and fresh mint leaves.
6. In a small bowl, whisk together tahini, fresh lemon juice, minced garlic, salt, and black pepper to create the lemon-tahini dressing.
7. Pour the lemon-tahini dressing over the quinoa and chickpea salad. Toss to combine.
8. Once the chickpeas are done, remove them from the air fryer and let them cool slightly.
9. Sprinkle the crispy chickpeas over the salad.
10. Serve the Quinoa and Chickpea Salad with Lemon-Tahini Dressing as a refreshing and healthy dish.

Pinto Bean and Green Chilli Fritters

Prep Time: 15 minutes / Cook Time: 10 minutes
Servings: 2 / Mode: Max Crisp

Ingredients:

- 1 can pinto beans, drained and rinsed
- Green Chillies, chopped
- Cornmeal • Fresh cilantro, chopped
- Ground cumin • Chilli powder
- Salt and black pepper, to taste
- Olive oil (for cooking)

Preparation Instructions:

1. Preheat your dual zone air fryer to Max Crisp mode.
2. In a food processor, combine pinto beans, chopped green Chillies, cornmeal, fresh cilantro, ground cumin, Chilli powder, salt, and black pepper. Pulse until the mixture is well combined but still slightly chunky.
3. Form the mixture into small fritters.
4. Brush or spray the fritters with a bit of olive oil.
5. Place the fritters in the preheated air fryer using Max Crisp mode. Cook for about 8-10 minutes, flipping halfway through, until they are crispy and golden brown.

6. Once done, transfer the Pinto Bean and Green Chilli Fritters to serving plates.
7. Serve the fritters hot.

Brown Rice and Kale Stuffed Cabbage Rolls

Prep Time: 30 minutes / Cook Time: 45 minutes
Servings: 4 / Mode: Bake

Ingredients:
- 8 large cabbage leaves
- 185g brown rice, cooked
- 60g kale, chopped and blanched
- 1 small onion, finely chopped
- 2 cloves garlic, minced
- 1 can (400g) diced tomatoes
- 1 teaspoon Italian seasoning
- Salt and black pepper, to taste
- Olive oil (for cooking)
- Grated Parmesan cheese (optional, for garnish)

Preparation Instructions:
1. Preheat your dual zone air fryer to 375°F using the Bake mode.
2. In a large pot of boiling water, blanch the cabbage leaves for 2-3 minutes or until they are pliable. Drain and set aside.
3. In a skillet, heat olive oil over medium heat. Add chopped onion and minced garlic. Sauté until the onion is translucent.
4. Stir in the diced tomatoes, Italian seasoning, salt, and black pepper. Cook for 5-7 minutes until the sauce thickens slightly.
5. In a mixing bowl, combine cooked brown rice, chopped kale, and half of the tomato sauce mixture. Mix well.
6. Place a cabbage leaf on a flat surface and spoon some of the rice and kale mixture onto the centre of the leaf. Roll up the cabbage leaf, tucking in the sides, to form a roll. Repeat with the remaining cabbage leaves.
7. Place the stuffed cabbage rolls in the preheated air fryer using the Bake mode. Cook for about 30-35 minutes until the cabbage is tender and the rolls are heated through.
8. Serve the Brown Rice and Kale Stuffed Cabbage Rolls hot, garnished with grated Parmesan cheese if desired.

Israeli Couscous with Roasted Vegetables

Prep Time: 15 minutes / Cook Time: 25 minutes
Servings: 4 / Mode: Roast

Ingredients:
- 185g couscous
- 340g mixed vegetables (e.g., bell peppers, zucchini, cherry tomatoes), diced
- 2 tablespoons olive oil
- 2 cloves garlic, minced
- 1 teaspoon dried oregano
- Salt and black pepper, to taste
- Fresh basil leaves (for garnish)

Preparation Instructions:
1. Preheat your dual zone air fryer to 375°F using the Roast mode.
2. In a bowl, toss the diced mixed vegetables with olive oil, minced garlic, dried oregano, salt, and black pepper.
3. Place the seasoned vegetables in the preheated air fryer using the Roast mode. Cook for about 20-25 minutes, stirring occasionally, until the vegetables are roasted and tender.
4. While the vegetables are roasting, cook the Israeli couscous according to the package instructions.
5. Once both the couscous and roasted vegetables are done, combine them in a large serving bowl.
6. Garnish with fresh basil leaves.
7. Serve the Israeli Couscous with Roasted Vegetables as a delightful dish.

Sorghum and Vegetable Pilaf

Prep Time: 20 minutes / Cook Time: 30 minutes
Servings: 4 / Mode: Air Fry

Ingredients:
- 185g sorghum, cooked
- 340g mixed vegetables (e.g., carrots, peas, corn), diced
- 1 small onion, finely chopped
- 2 cloves garlic, minced
- 2 tablespoons olive oil
- 1 teaspoon ground cumin
- 1/2 teaspoon ground coriander
- Salt and black pepper, to taste
- Fresh cilantro leaves (for garnish)

Preparation Instructions:
1. Preheat your dual zone air fryer to 350°F using the Air Fry mode.
2. In a skillet, heat olive oil over medium heat. Add chopped onion and minced garlic. Sauté until the onion is translucent.
3. Stir in the diced mixed vegetables, ground cumin, ground coriander, salt, and black pepper. Cook for 5-7 minutes until the vegetables are tender.
4. Add the cooked sorghum to the skillet and toss to

combine. Cook for an additional 5 minutes to heat through.

5. Transfer the Sorghum and Vegetable Pilaf to a serving dish.
6. Garnish with fresh cilantro leaves.
7. Serve the pilaf as a hearty and nutritious side dish.

Thai Pineapple Coconut Rice

Prep Time: 15 minutes / Cook Time: 30 minutes
Servings: 4 / Mode: Air Fry

Ingredients:

- 200g jasmine rice
- 400ml coconut milk
- 200ml pineapple juice
- 200g fresh pineapple chunks
- 1 red bell pepper, diced
- 1 small onion, finely chopped
- 2 cloves garlic, minced
- 30ml vegetable oil
- 10g fresh cilantro, chopped (for garnish)
- Salt and black pepper, to taste

Preparation Instructions:

1. Preheat your dual zone air fryer to 350°F using the Air Fry mode.
2. In a saucepan, combine jasmine rice, coconut milk, and pineapple juice. Bring to a boil, then reduce the heat to low, cover, and simmer for 15-20 minutes, or until the rice is cooked and the liquid is absorbed.
3. While the rice is cooking, heat vegetable oil in a skillet over medium heat. Add chopped onion and minced garlic. Sauté until the onion is translucent.
4. Stir in diced red bell pepper and fresh pineapple chunks. Cook for an additional 5-7 minutes until the pineapple and bell pepper are tender.
5. Once the rice is done, fluff it with a fork and combine it with the sautéed pineapple and bell pepper mixture.
6. Season with salt and black pepper to taste.
7. Transfer the Thai Pineapple Coconut Rice to serving plates.
8. Garnish with chopped fresh cilantro.
9. Serve the flavorful Thai Pineapple Coconut Rice as a delicious side dish or main course.

Butter Bean and Tomato Hash

Prep Time: 15 minutes / Cook Time: 20 minutes
Servings: 4 / Mode: Roast

Ingredients:

- 400g butter beans, cooked and drained
- 400g cherry tomatoes, halved
- 1 red onion, thinly sliced
- 2 cloves garlic, minced
- 30ml olive oil
- 5g fresh thyme leaves
- Salt and black pepper, to taste
- Fresh parsley, chopped (for garnish)

Preparation Instructions:

1. Preheat your dual zone air fryer to 375°F using the Roast mode.
2. In a large mixing bowl, combine cooked butter beans, halved cherry tomatoes, thinly sliced red onion, minced garlic, olive oil, fresh thyme leaves, salt, and black pepper. Toss to coat.
3. Spread the mixture evenly in the preheated air fryer using the Roast mode.
4. Roast for about 15-20 minutes, stirring occasionally, until the tomatoes are softened and slightly caramelised.
5. Once done, transfer the Butter Bean and Tomato Hash to serving plates.
6. Garnish with chopped fresh parsley.
7. Serve the flavorful Butter Bean and Tomato Hash as a tasty and nutritious side dish.

Barley and Roasted Beet Salad

Prep Time: 15 minutes / Cook Time: 30 minutes
Servings: 4 / Mode: Bake

Ingredients:

- 200g pearl barley, cooked and cooled
- 400g roasted beets, diced
- 200g cucumber, diced
- 200g cherry tomatoes, halved
- 1 small red onion, finely chopped
- 30ml olive oil
- 30ml balsamic vinegar
- 10g fresh basil leaves, chopped
- Salt and black pepper, to taste

Preparation Instructions:

1. Preheat your dual zone air fryer to 375°F using the Bake mode.
2. In a large mixing bowl, combine cooked and cooled pearl barley, diced roasted beets, diced cucumber, halved cherry tomatoes, and finely chopped red onion.
3. In a separate bowl, whisk together olive oil, balsamic vinegar, chopped fresh basil leaves, salt, and black pepper to create the dressing.
4. Pour the dressing over the barley and vegetable mixture. Toss to coat.
5. Transfer the Barley and Roasted Beet Salad to serving plates.
6. Serve this vibrant and healthy salad as a delicious

side or a light main course.

Fava Bean and Mint Falafel

Prep Time: 15 minutes / Cook Time: 15 minutes
Servings: 4 / Mode: Air Fry

Ingredients:

- 200g dried fava beans, soaked and cooked
- 1 small onion, finely chopped
- 2 cloves garlic, minced
- 15g fresh mint leaves
- 5g ground cumin
- 5g ground coriander
- 5g baking powder
- Salt and black pepper, to taste
- Vegetable oil (for brushing)

Preparation Instructions:

1. Preheat your dual zone air fryer to 375°F using the Air Fry mode.
2. In a food processor, combine cooked fava beans, chopped onion, minced garlic, fresh mint leaves, ground cumin, ground coriander, baking powder, salt, and black pepper. Pulse until the mixture is well combined but still slightly coarse.
3. Form the mixture into small falafel patties or balls.
4. Brush the falafel patties with a little vegetable oil.
5. Place the falafel in the preheated air fryer using the Air Fry mode. Cook for about 12-15 minutes, turning them halfway through, until they are golden brown and crispy.
6. Remove the Fava Bean and Mint Falafel from the air fryer.
7. Serve the falafel hot with your favourite sauce or dip.

Mung Bean and Spinach Crepes

Prep Time: 15 minutes / Cook Time: 20 minutes
Servings: 4 / Mode: Roast

Ingredients:

- For the Crepes:
- 200g mung bean flour
- 5g salt
- 30ml vegetable oil
- 300ml water
- 5g ground turmeric
- For the Filling:
- 200g fresh spinach leaves
- 1 small onion, finely chopped
- 2 cloves garlic, minced
- 5g ground cumin
- 5g ground coriander
- Salt and black pepper, to taste

Preparation Instructions:

1. Preheat your dual zone air fryer to 375°F using the

Roast mode.
2. In a bowl, whisk together mung bean flour, water, salt, and ground turmeric to make the crepe batter.
3. Grease a non-stick skillet with a bit of vegetable oil and heat it over medium-high heat. Pour a ladleful of the crepe batter into the skillet, swirling it to cover the bottom evenly. Cook until the edges lift and the crepe is set, then flip and cook briefly on the other side. Repeat until you've made all the crepes.
4. In a separate skillet, heat vegetable oil over medium heat. Add chopped onion and minced garlic. Sauté until the onion is translucent.
5. Stir in fresh spinach leaves, ground cumin, ground coriander, salt, and black pepper. Cook until the spinach wilts and is tender.
6. Place a spoonful of the spinach mixture in the centre of each crepe, fold the sides over, and roll them up.
7. Transfer the Mung Bean and Spinach Crepes to the preheated air fryer using the Roast mode. Cook for about 5 minutes to heat through.
8. Serve the crepes hot and enjoy this healthy and flavorful dish.

Thai Basil Fried Rice with Tofu

Prep Time: 15 minutes / Cook Time: 20 minutes
Servings: 4 / Mode: Air Fry

Ingredients:

- 200g cooked jasmine rice, cooled
- 200g extra-firm tofu, cubed
- 2 cloves garlic, minced
- 1 red bell pepper, diced
- 1 small carrot, diced
- 10g fresh basil leaves
- 60ml soy sauce
- 30ml vegetable oil
- Fresh cilantro leaves (for garnish)
- Lime wedges (for serving)

Preparation Instructions:

1. Preheat your dual zone air fryer to 375°F using the Air Fry mode.
2. In a wok or skillet, heat vegetable oil over medium-high heat. Add cubed tofu and stir-fry until it becomes golden brown and crispy. Remove from the wok and set aside.
3. In the same wok, add minced garlic, diced red bell pepper, and diced carrot. Stir-fry for a few minutes until the vegetables are tender.
4. Add cooked jasmine rice and cooked tofu to the wok. Pour in soy sauce and stir-fry for another 5-7 minutes, ensuring everything is well mixed.
5. Tear the fresh basil leaves and add them to the Thai Basil Fried Rice. Stir-fry for another 2 minutes.
6. Transfer the fried rice to serving plates.

7. Garnish with fresh cilantro leaves and serve with lime wedges.
8. Enjoy this aromatic and savoury Thai Basil Fried Rice with Tofu with the family.

Mexican Street Corn Rice

Prep Time: 15 minutes / Cook Time: 20 minutes
Servings: 4 / Mode: Roast

Ingredients:

- 200g long-grain white rice, cooked and cooled
- 250g corn kernels (fresh or frozen)
- 30ml mayonnaise
- 15ml sour cream
- 30g Cotija cheese, crumbled (or feta cheese)
- 5g chilli powder
- 5g paprika
- 10g fresh cilantro leaves, chopped (for garnish)
- Lime wedges (for serving)
- Salt and black pepper, to taste

Preparation Instructions:

1. Preheat your dual zone air fryer to 375°F using the Roast mode.
2. In a mixing bowl, combine cooked white rice and corn kernels.
3. In a separate bowl, whisk together mayonnaise, sour cream, crumbled Cotija cheese, Chilli powder, and paprika. Season with salt and black pepper to taste.
4. Pour the mayo mixture over the rice and corn mixture. Stir to coat evenly.
5. Transfer the Mexican Street Corn Rice to the preheated air fryer using the Roast mode. Roast for about 10-12 minutes, stirring occasionally, until the rice is heated through and slightly crispy.
6. Remove from the air fryer and garnish with fresh cilantro leaves.
7. Serve the Mexican Street Corn Rice with lime wedges for an extra zesty touch.

Cuban Black Beans and Rice

Prep Time: 15 minutes / Cook Time: 30 minutes
Servings: 4 / Mode: Air Fry

Ingredients:

- 200g long-grain white rice
- 400g canned black beans, drained and rinsed
- 1 small onion, finely chopped
- 2 cloves garlic, minced
- 5g ground cumin
- 5g dried oregano
- 30ml olive oil
- 30ml white vinegar
- Fresh cilantro leaves (for garnish)
- Salt and black pepper, to taste

Preparation Instructions:

1. Preheat your dual zone air fryer to 375°F using the Air Fry mode.
2. In a saucepan, cook the white rice according to package instructions. Fluff with a fork and set aside.
3. In a skillet, heat olive oil over medium heat. Add chopped onion and minced garlic. Sauté until the onion is translucent.
4. Stir in ground cumin, dried oregano, and drained black beans. Cook for another 5 minutes until heated through.
5. Add cooked white rice to the bean mixture. Pour in white vinegar and stir to combine. Cook for an additional 5-7 minutes until everything is well mixed.
6. Season with salt and black pepper to taste.
7. Transfer the Cuban Black Beans and Rice to serving plates.
8. Garnish with fresh cilantro leaves.
9. Serve this flavorful Cuban dish as a satisfying and wholesome meal.

Mushroom and Thyme Farro Risotto

Prep Time: 15 minutes / Cook Time: 30 minutes
Servings: 4 / Mode: Bake

Ingredients:

- 200g farro, cooked
- 250g cremini mushrooms, sliced
- 1 small onion, finely chopped
- 2 cloves garlic, minced
- 30ml olive oil   • 10g fresh thyme leaves
- 60ml dry white wine • 60ml vegetable broth
- 30g Parmesan cheese, grated
- Salt and black pepper, to taste

Preparation Instructions:

1. Preheat your dual zone air fryer to 375°F using the Bake mode.
2. In a skillet, heat olive oil over medium heat. Add chopped onion and sliced cremini mushrooms. Sauté until the mushrooms are golden brown.
3. Stir in minced garlic and fresh thyme leaves. Cook for another minute.
4. Pour in dry white wine and cook until it's mostly absorbed.
5. Add cooked farro to the mushroom mixture. Pour in vegetable broth and stir well. Cook for an additional 5-7 minutes, allowing the flavors to meld.
6. Stir in grated Parmesan cheese and season with salt and black pepper to taste.

7. Transfer the Mushroom and Thyme Farro Risotto to serving plates.
8. Serve this rich and savoury risotto as a comforting and satisfying meal.

Millet and Sweet Potato Patties

Prep Time: 20 minutes / Cook Time: 20 minutes
Servings: 4 / Mode: Air Fry

Ingredients:

- 200g millet, cooked and cooled
- 300g sweet potatoes, cooked and mashed
- 1 small onion, finely chopped
- 2 cloves garlic, minced
- 5g smoked paprika
- 30g grated Parmesan cheese
- 5g ground cumin
- 30g breadcrumbs
- 1 egg
- Salt and black pepper, to taste
- Vegetable oil (for brushing)

Preparation Instructions:

1. Preheat your dual zone air fryer to 375°F using the Air Fry mode.
2. In a large bowl, combine cooked millet, mashed sweet potatoes, chopped onion, minced garlic, ground cumin, smoked paprika, breadcrumbs, grated Parmesan cheese, and one egg. Mix until the ingredients are well combined.
3. Season the mixture with salt and black pepper to taste.
4. Form the mixture into patties.
5. Brush the patties with a little vegetable oil.
6. Place the patties in the preheated air fryer using the Air Fry mode. Cook for about 15-20 minutes, turning them halfway through, until they are golden brown and crispy.
7. Remove the Millet and Sweet Potato Patties from the air fryer.
8. Serve the patties hot with your choice of sauce or condiments.

Spicy Black Bean Tostadas

Prep Time: 15 minutes / Cook Time: 10 minutes
Servings: 4 / Mode: Roast

Ingredients:

- 400g canned black beans, drained and rinsed
- 4 corn tortillas
- 1 small red onion, thinly sliced
- 1 jalapeño pepper, thinly sliced
- 60g grated Cheddar cheese
- 30ml hot sauce
- 15ml lime juice
- Fresh cilantro leaves (for garnish)
- Salt and black pepper, to taste

Preparation Instructions:

1. Preheat your dual zone air fryer to 375°F using the Roast mode.
2. Place corn tortillas in the preheated air fryer using the Roast mode. Roast for about 5 minutes until they become slightly crispy.
3. In a bowl, combine drained black beans, thinly sliced red onion, thinly sliced jalapeño pepper, hot sauce, lime juice, salt, and black pepper. Mix until well combined.
4. Remove the tortillas from the air fryer.
5. Spread the black bean mixture evenly on each tortilla.
6. Top with grated Cheddar cheese.
7. Place the assembled tostadas back in the air fryer using the Roast mode. Roast for another 5 minutes until the cheese is melted and bubbly.
8. Garnish with fresh cilantro leaves.
9. Serve the Spicy Black Bean Tostadas hot for a flavorful meal.

Herbed Couscous with Roasted Vegetables

Prep Time: 15 minutes / Cook Time: 20 minutes
Servings: 4 / Mode: Bake

Ingredients:

- 200g couscous
- 400g mixed vegetables (zucchini, bell peppers, cherry tomatoes)
- 30ml olive oil
- 5g dried basil
- 5g dried oregano
- 5g dried thyme
- Salt and black pepper, to taste
- Fresh parsley leaves (for garnish)

Preparation Instructions:

1. Preheat your dual zone air fryer to 375°F using the Bake mode.
2. In a large bowl, toss mixed vegetables with olive oil, dried oregano, dried basil, dried thyme, salt, and black pepper.
3. Spread the seasoned vegetables in the preheated air fryer using the Bake mode. Bake for about 15-20 minutes until they are roasted and tender.
4. While the vegetables are roasting, prepare couscous according to package instructions.
5. Fluff the cooked couscous with a fork.
6. Once the vegetables are done, combine them with the cooked couscous in a large bowl.
7. Garnish with fresh parsley leaves.
8. Serve the Herbed Couscous with Roasted Vegetables as a delightful and healthy dish.

Chapter 8 Fish and SeaFood

Crab Cakes with Remoulade Sauce

Prep Time: 20 minutes / Cook Time: 10 minutes
Servings: 4 / Mode: Air Fry

Ingredients:

- For the Crab Cakes:
- 400g lump crabmeat, drained and picked over
- Breadcrumbs
- Mayonnaise
- 1 egg, beaten
- Dijon mustard
- Old Bay seasoning
- Worcestershire sauce
- Salt and black pepper, to taste
- For the Remoulade Sauce:
- Mayonnaise
- Dijon mustard
- Capers, chopped
- Gherkins or pickles, chopped
- Fresh lemon juice
- Paprika
- Salt and black pepper, to taste

Preparation Instructions:

1. Preheat your dual zone air fryer to 375°F using the Air Fry mode.
2. In a bowl, combine lump crabmeat, breadcrumbs, mayonnaise, beaten egg, Dijon mustard, Old Bay seasoning, Worcestershire sauce, salt, and black pepper. Mix until well combined.
3. Form the mixture into crab cakes, shaping them to your desired size.
4. Place the crab cakes in the preheated air fryer using the Air Fry mode. Cook for about 10 minutes or until they are golden brown and cooked through, flipping halfway through.
5. While the crab cakes are cooking, prepare the Remoulade sauce. In a separate bowl, combine mayonnaise, Dijon mustard, capers, gherkins, lemon juice, paprika, salt, and black pepper. Mix until smooth.
6. Serve the hot Crab Cakes with the Remoulade Sauce on the side for dipping.

Turbot with Brown Butter and Capers

Prep Time: 15 minutes / Cook Time: 10 minutes
Servings: 2 / Mode: Roast

Ingredients:

- 2 turbot fillets (about 200g each)
- Salt and black pepper, to taste
- 2 tablespoons olive oil
- 30g unsalted butter
- 1 tablespoon capers, drained
- 1 tablespoon fresh lemon juice
- Fresh parsley, chopped (for garnish)

Preparation Instructions:

1. Preheat your dual zone air fryer to 375°F using the Roast mode.
2. Season the turbot fillets with salt and black pepper.
3. Drizzle olive oil over the turbot fillets.
4. Place the turbot fillets in the preheated air fryer using the Roast mode. Cook for about 8-10 minutes or until the fillets are cooked through and flake easily with a fork.
5. While the turbot is cooking, melt the unsalted butter in a small saucepan over medium heat. Cook until the butter turns golden brown and develops a nutty aroma, about 3-4 minutes. Remove from heat.
6. Stir in the capers and fresh lemon juice into the browned butter.
7. Once the turbot fillets are done, transfer them to serving plates.
8. Drizzle the brown butter and caper sauce over the turbot fillets.
9. Garnish with chopped fresh parsley.
10. Serve the Turbot with Brown Butter and Capers hot.

Whiting Fillets with Lemon Herb Sauce

Prep Time: 15 minutes / Cook Time: 10 minutes
Servings: 4 / Mode: Bake

Ingredients:

- Whiting fillets

- Zest and juice of 1 lemon
- 2 tablespoons fresh parsley, chopped
- 1 teaspoon fresh thyme leaves
- 2 cloves garlic, minced
- 2 tablespoons olive oil
- Salt and black pepper, to taste

Preparation Instructions:

1. Preheat your dual zone air fryer to 375°F using the Bake mode.
2. In a bowl, combine lemon zest, lemon juice, fresh parsley, fresh thyme leaves, minced garlic, olive oil, salt, and black pepper to create a lemon herb sauce.
3. Place the whiting fillets in the preheated air fryer using the Bake mode. Cook for about 8-10 minutes or until the fillets are cooked through and flake easily with a fork.
4. Drizzle the lemon herb sauce over the cooked whiting fillets.
5. Serve the Whiting Fillets with Lemon Herb Sauce hot as a flavorful seafood dish.

Coconut-Crusted Cod with Pineapple Salsa

Prep Time: 20 minutes / Cook Time: 15 minutes
Servings: 2 / Mode: Bake

Ingredients:

- For the Coconut-Crusted Cod:
- 2 cod fillets (about 200g each)
- 50g shredded coconut
- 50g breadcrumbs
- Salt and black pepper, to taste
- 1 egg, beaten
- Olive oil (for brushing)
- For the Pineapple Salsa:
- 240g fresh pineapple, diced
- 60g red onion, finely chopped
- 15g fresh cilantro, chopped
- 30ml lime juice
- 1/2 jalapeño pepper, minced (adjust to your spice preference)
- Juice of 1 lime
- Salt and black pepper, to taste

Preparation Instructions:

1. Preheat your dual zone air fryer to 375°F using the Bake mode.
2. In a shallow dish, combine shredded coconut, breadcrumbs, salt, and black pepper.
3. Dip each cod fillet into the beaten egg, allowing any excess to drip off, and then coat with the coconut-breadcrumb mixture.
4. Place the coconut-crusted cod fillets in the preheated air fryer using the Bake mode. Cook for about 12-15 minutes or until the cod is cooked through and the crust is golden brown and crispy.
5. While the cod is cooking, prepare the Pineapple Salsa. In a bowl, combine diced fresh pineapple, finely chopped red onion, fresh cilantro, minced jalapeño pepper, lime juice, salt, and black pepper. Mix well.
6. Once the cod is done, transfer it to serving plates.
7. Top each cod fillet with a generous spoonful of Pineapple Salsa.
8. Serve the Coconut-Crusted Cod with Pineapple Salsa hot and enjoy a delicious meal.

Miso-Glazed Sea Bass

Prep Time: 15 minutes / Cook Time: 15 minutes
Servings: 2 / Mode: Roast

Ingredients:

- 2 sea bass fillets (about 200g each)
- 2 tablespoons white miso paste
- 1 tablespoon mirin
- 1 tablespoon sake
- 1 tablespoon sugar
- 1 tablespoon soy sauce
- 1 teaspoon fresh ginger, minced
- 1 clove garlic, minced
- Black sesame seeds (for garnish)
- Sliced green onions (for garnish)

Preparation Instructions:

1. Preheat your dual zone air fryer to 375°F using the Roast mode.
2. In a bowl, whisk together white miso paste, mirin, sake, sugar, soy sauce, minced ginger, and minced garlic to create the miso glaze.
3. Place the sea bass fillets in the preheated air fryer using the Roast mode. Cook for about 12-15 minutes or until the sea bass is cooked through and the glaze has caramelised.
4. Once the sea bass is done, transfer it to serving plates.
5. Garnish with black sesame seeds and sliced green onions.
6. Serve the Miso-Glazed Sea Bass hot.

Spiced Sea Bream

Prep Time: 20 minutes / Cook Time: 15 minutes
Servings: 2 / Mode: Max Crisp

Ingredients:

- 2 sea bream fillets (about 200g each)
- 1 teaspoon ground cumin
- 1 teaspoon ground coriander
- 1/2 teaspoon paprika
- Salt and black pepper, to taste
- Olive oil (for brushing)

Preparation Instructions:

1. Preheat your dual zone air fryer to Max Crisp mode.
2. In a small bowl, combine ground cumin, ground coriander, paprika, salt, and black pepper.
3. Rub the spice mixture evenly over both sides of the sea bream fillets.
4. Brush the fillets with a little olive oil.
5. Place the sea bream fillets in the preheated air fryer using Max Crisp mode. Cook for about 12-15 minutes or until the fillets are cooked through and the skin is crispy.
6. Once the sea bream is done, transfer it to serving plates.
7. Serve the Spiced Sea Bream hot and enjoy!

Salted Hake Fillets

Prep Time: 15 minutes / Cook Time: 10 minutes
Servings: 2 / Mode: Bake

Ingredients:

- 2 hake fillets (about 200g each)
- Salt, to taste
- Olive oil (for brushing)

Preparation Instructions:

1. Preheat your dual zone air fryer to 375°F using the Bake mode.
2. Season the hake fillets with a sprinkle of salt.
3. Brush the fillets with a little olive oil.
4. Place the hake fillets in the preheated air fryer using the Bake mode. Cook for about 8-10 minutes or until the fillets are cooked through and flake easily with a fork.
5. Once the hake fillets are done, transfer them to serving plates.
6. Serve the Salted Hake Fillets hot for a simple and delicious seafood dish.

Smoked Trout and Watercress Quiche

Prep Time: 20 minutes / Cook Time: 30 minutes
Servings: 4 / Mode: Bake

Ingredients:

- 1 pie crust
- 200g smoked trout, flaked
- 25g watercress leaves
- 4 eggs
- 200ml heavy cream
- Salt and black pepper, to taste
- Nutmeg, a pinch (optional)

Preparation Instructions:

1. Preheat your dual zone air fryer to 375°F using the Bake mode.
2. Lay the pie crust in a baking dish.
3. Spread the flaked smoked trout and watercress leaves over the pie crust.
4. In a bowl, whisk together eggs and heavy cream. Season with salt, black pepper, and a pinch of nutmeg if desired.
5. Pour the egg and cream mixture over the trout and watercress.
6. Place the quiche in the preheated air fryer using the Bake mode. Cook for about 25-30 minutes or until the quiche is set and the top is lightly browned.
7. Once done, remove the quiche from the air fryer and let it cool slightly before slicing.
8. Serve the Smoked Trout and Watercress Quiche warm or at room temperature.

Tamarind-Glazed Mahi-Mahi

Prep Time: 15 minutes / Cook Time: 15 minutes
Servings: 2 / Mode: Roast

Ingredients:

- 2 Mahi-Mahi fillets (about 200g each)
- 2 tablespoons tamarind paste
- 2 tablespoons honey
- 1 tablespoon soy sauce
- 1 teaspoon fresh ginger, minced
- 1 clove garlic, minced
- Salt and black pepper, to taste
- Fresh cilantro leaves (for garnish)

Preparation Instructions:

1. Preheat your dual zone air fryer to 375°F using the

Roast mode.

2. In a bowl, whisk together tamarind paste, honey, soy sauce, minced ginger, minced garlic, salt, and black pepper to create the tamarind glaze.
3. Brush the Mahi-Mahi fillets with the tamarind glaze, reserving some for later.
4. Place the Mahi-Mahi fillets in the preheated air fryer using the Roast mode. Cook for about 12-15 minutes or until the fillets are cooked through.
5. While the Mahi-Mahi is cooking, heat the reserved tamarind glaze in a saucepan until it thickens slightly.
6. Once the Mahi-Mahi fillets are done, transfer them to serving plates.
7. Drizzle the thickened tamarind glaze over the fillets.
8. Garnish with fresh cilantro leaves.
9. Serve the Tamarind-Glazed Mahi-Mahi hot as a flavorful seafood dish.

Herring with Mustard Sauce

Prep Time: 15 minutes / Cook Time: 10 minutes
Servings: 2 / Mode: Max Crisp

Ingredients:
- 2 herring fillets
- Salt and black pepper, to taste
- 2 tablespoons Dijon mustard
- 1 tablespoon whole-grain mustard
- 2 tablespoons sour cream
- 1 tablespoon fresh dill, chopped
- Lemon wedges (for serving)

Preparation Instructions:
1. Preheat your dual zone air fryer to Max Crisp mode.
2. Season the herring fillets with salt and black pepper.
3. In a bowl, mix together Dijon mustard, whole-grain mustard, sour cream, and fresh dill to create the mustard sauce.
4. Place the herring fillets in the preheated air fryer using Max Crisp mode. Cook for about 8-10 minutes or until the fillets are cooked through and the skin is crispy.
5. Once done, transfer the herring fillets to serving plates.
6. Drizzle the mustard sauce over the herring fillets.
7. Serve the Herring with Mustard Sauce hot with lemon wedges on the side.

Blackened Catfish

Prep Time: 10 minutes / Cook Time: 10 minutes
Servings: 2 / Mode: Roast

Ingredients:
- 2 catfish fillets
- 1 tablespoon paprika
- 1/2 teaspoon dried thyme
- 1/2 teaspoon dried oregano
- 1/2 teaspoon garlic powder
- 1/2 teaspoon onion powder
- 1/2 teaspoon cayenne pepper (adjust to your spice preference)
- 1/2 teaspoon salt
- 1/4 teaspoon black pepper
- Olive oil (for brushing)

Preparation Instructions:
1. Preheat your dual zone air fryer to 375°F using the Roast mode.
2. In a small bowl, combine paprika, dried thyme, dried oregano, garlic powder, onion powder, cayenne pepper, salt, and black pepper to create the blackening spice mix.
3. Brush the catfish fillets with a little olive oil.
4. Rub the blackening spice mix evenly over both sides of the catfish fillets.
5. Place the catfish fillets in the preheated air fryer using the Roast mode. Cook for about 8-10 minutes or until the catfish is cooked through and has a blackened crust.
6. Once done, transfer the blackened catfish to serving plates.
7. Serve the Blackened Catfish hot for a flavorful seafood dish.

Szechuan-Style Tilapia

Prep Time: 15 minutes / Cook Time: 15 minutes
Servings: 2 / Mode: Bake

Ingredients:
- 2 tilapia fillets (about 200g each)
- 2 tablespoons soy sauce
- 1 tablespoon rice vinegar
- 1 tablespoon honey
- 1 teaspoon Szechuan peppercorns, crushed (adjust to your spice preference)
- 1/2 teaspoon fresh ginger, minced
- 1/2 teaspoon garlic, minced

- Green onions, chopped (for garnish)
- Sesame seeds (for garnish)

Preparation Instructions:

1. Preheat your dual zone air fryer to 375°F using the Bake mode.
2. In a bowl, whisk together soy sauce, rice vinegar, honey, crushed Szechuan peppercorns, minced ginger, and minced garlic to create the Szechuan-style marinade.
3. Place the tilapia fillets in the marinade and let them marinate for about 10 minutes.
4. Remove the tilapia fillets from the marinade and place them in the preheated air fryer using the Bake mode. Cook for about 12-15 minutes or until the tilapia is cooked through.
5. Once done, transfer the Szechuan-Style Tilapia to serving plates.
6. Garnish with chopped green onions and sesame seeds.
7. Serve the Szechuan-Style Tilapia hot for a spicy and flavorful seafood dish.

Turbot with Brown Butter and Capers

Prep Time: 15 minutes / Cook Time: 15 minutes
Servings: 2 / Mode: Roast

Ingredients:

- 2 turbot fillets (about 200g each)
- Salt and black pepper, to taste
- 2 tablespoons unsalted butter
- 1 tablespoon capers
- 1 tablespoon fresh lemon juice
- Fresh parsley, chopped (for garnish)
- Lemon wedges (for serving)

Preparation Instructions:

1. Preheat your dual zone air fryer to 375°F using the Roast mode.
2. Season the turbot fillets with salt and black pepper.
3. In a skillet, melt the unsalted butter over medium heat until it starts to brown.
4. Add the capers and fresh lemon juice to the browned butter. Stir well.

5. Place the turbot fillets in the preheated air fryer using the Roast mode. Cook for about 12-15 minutes or until the turbot is cooked through and has a golden brown crust.
6. Once done, transfer the turbot fillets to serving plates.
7. Drizzle the brown butter and caper sauce over the turbot fillets.
8. Garnish with chopped fresh parsley and serve with lemon wedges on the side.

Tuna Steak with Wasabi Mayo

Prep Time: 15 minutes / Cook Time: 10 minutes
Servings: 2 / Mode: Max Crisp

Ingredients:

- 2 tuna steaks (about 200g each)
- Salt and black pepper, to taste
- Olive oil (for brushing)
- 2 tablespoons mayonnaise
- 1 teaspoon wasabi paste (adjust to your spice preference)
- 1 teaspoon fresh lime juice
- 1/2 teaspoon soy sauce
- 1/2 teaspoon honey
- Lime wedges (for serving)

Preparation Instructions:

1. Preheat your dual zone air fryer to Max Crisp mode.
2. Season the tuna steaks with salt and black pepper.
3. Brush the tuna steaks with a little olive oil.
4. Place the tuna steaks in the preheated air fryer using Max Crisp mode. Cook for about 8-10 minutes, depending on your desired level of doneness (medium-rare to medium).
5. While the tuna is cooking, prepare the Wasabi Mayo. In a bowl, combine mayonnaise, wasabi paste, fresh lime juice, soy sauce, and honey. Mix well.
6. Once the tuna steaks are done, transfer them to serving plates.
7. Drizzle the Wasabi Mayo over the tuna steaks.
8. Serve the Tuna Steak with Wasabi Mayo hot, accompanied by lime wedges for added flavour.

Chapter 9 Beef, Pork and Lamb

Mongolian Beef Stir-Fry

Prep Time: 15 minutes / Cook Time: 15 minutes
Servings: 4 / Mode: Air Fry

Ingredients:
- 500g flank steak, thinly sliced
- 2 tablespoons vegetable oil
- 3 cloves garlic, minced
- 1 teaspoon fresh ginger, minced
- 120ml soy sauce
- 100g brown sugar
- 2 green onions, sliced
- Sesame seeds (for garnish)
- Steamed rice, for serving

Preparation Instructions:
1. Preheat your dual zone air fryer to 375°F using the Stir-Fry mode.
2. In a large skillet or wok, heat the vegetable oil over high heat. Add the sliced flank steak and stir-fry for about 2-3 minutes until browned. Remove from the skillet and set aside.
3. In the same skillet, add the minced garlic and ginger. Sauté for about 30 seconds until fragrant.
4. Pour in the soy sauce and brown sugar. Stir until the sugar has dissolved and the sauce thickens.
5. Return the cooked beef to the skillet and toss to coat it evenly with the sauce. Cook for an additional 2-3 minutes until the beef is heated through.
6. Serve the Mongolian Beef Stir-Fry hot, garnished with sliced green onions and sesame seeds. Serve over steamed rice.

Beef Satay with Peanut Sauce

Prep Time: 20 minutes / Cook Time: 10 minutes
Servings: 4 / Mode: Air Fry

Ingredients:
- For the Beef Satay:
- 500g beef sirloin, thinly sliced
- 2 tablespoons soy sauce
- 2 cloves garlic, minced
- 1 teaspoon ground cumin
- 1 teaspoon ground coriander
- 1 teaspoon turmeric
- Wooden skewers, soaked in water
- For the Peanut Sauce:
- 120g creamy peanut butter
- 60ml coconut milk
- 2 tablespoons soy sauce
- 1 tablespoon brown sugar
- 1 tablespoon lime juice
- 1 clove garlic, minced

Preparation Instructions:
1. Preheat your dual zone air fryer to 375°F using the Air Fry mode.
2. In a bowl, combine the soy sauce, minced garlic, ground cumin, ground coriander, and turmeric. Marinate the sliced beef in this mixture for about 10 minutes.
3. Thread the marinated beef slices onto the soaked wooden skewers.
4. Place the beef skewers in the preheated air fryer using the Air Fry mode. Cook for about 5 minutes, turning halfway through, until the beef is cooked to your desired level of doneness.
5. While the beef is cooking, prepare the peanut sauce. In a small saucepan, combine the peanut butter, coconut milk, soy sauce, brown sugar, lime juice, and minced garlic. Heat over low heat, stirring until the sauce is smooth and heated through.
6. Serve the Beef Satay hot with the warm Peanut Sauce for dipping.

Pork Cheek Terrine

Prep Time: 20 minutes / Cook Time: 40 minutes
Servings: 6 / Mode: Bake

Ingredients:
- 500g pork cheeks
- 1 carrot, chopped
- 1 onion, chopped
- 2 cloves garlic, minced
- 2 sprigs fresh thyme
- 120ml white wine
- 240ml chicken stock
- Salt and black pepper, to taste

Preparation Instructions:
1. Preheat your dual zone air fryer to 375°F using the Bake mode.
2. In a large skillet, heat a bit of oil over medium-high heat. Add the pork cheeks and sear them until browned on all sides. Remove and set aside.

3. In the same skillet, add the chopped carrot, onion, and minced garlic. Sauté for about 5 minutes until softened.
4. Return the seared pork cheeks to the skillet. Add the fresh thyme, white wine, and chicken stock. Season with salt and black pepper.
5. Transfer the mixture to an ovenproof dish and cover it with aluminium foil.
6. Bake in the preheated air fryer using the Bake mode for about 40 minutes or until the pork cheeks are tender and cooked through.
7. Remove from the air fryer and let it cool.
8. Once cooled, slice the Pork Cheek Terrine and serve.

Sticky Chinese BBQ Pork Ribs

Prep Time: 15 minutes / Cook Time: 30 minutes
Servings: 4 / Mode: Roast

Ingredients:
- For the Marinade:
- 500g pork ribs
- 60ml hoisin sauce
- 60ml soy sauce
- 30ml honey
- 2 cloves garlic, minced
- 2 teaspoons Chinese five-spice powder
- 1 teaspoon ginger, grated
- For the Glaze:
- 60ml honey
- 15ml soy sauce
- 1 teaspoon sesame oil
- 1 teaspoon rice vinegar

Preparation Instructions:
1. Preheat your dual zone air fryer to 375°F using the Roast mode.
2. In a bowl, combine all the marinade ingredients. Add the pork ribs and coat them evenly. Let them marinate for at least 15 minutes.
3. Place the marinated pork ribs in the preheated air fryer using the Roast mode. Cook for about 30 minutes, turning occasionally, until the ribs are cooked through and sticky.
4. While the ribs are cooking, prepare the glaze by combining honey, soy sauce, sesame oil, and rice vinegar in a small saucepan. Heat over low heat until warmed through.
5. Brush the cooked ribs with the glaze during the last 5 minutes of cooking.
6. Serve the Sticky Chinese BBQ Pork Ribs hot,

garnished with sesame seeds and chopped green onions.

Pork and Cider-Stuffed Bell Peppers

Prep Time: 20 minutes / Cook Time: 30 minutes
Servings: 4 / Mode: Bake

Ingredients:
- 4 large bell peppers, any colour
- 400g ground pork
- 1 onion, chopped
- 2 cloves garlic, minced
- 240ml tomato sauce
- 120ml apple cider
- 120g cooked rice
- 1 teaspoon dried oregano
- Salt and black pepper, to taste
- Grated cheese (for topping)
- Fresh parsley leaves (for garnish)

Preparation Instructions:
1. Preheat your dual zone air fryer to 375°F using the Bake mode.
2. Cut the tops off the bell peppers and remove the seeds and membranes. Set aside.
3. In a skillet, cook the ground pork over medium heat until browned. Drain any excess fat.
4. Add chopped onion and minced garlic to the skillet. Cook for about 3 minutes until the onion is soft.
5. Stir in the tomato sauce, apple cider, cooked rice, dried oregano, salt, and black pepper. Simmer for about 5 minutes.
6. Fill each bell pepper with the pork and rice mixture.
7. Place the stuffed bell peppers in the preheated air fryer using the Bake mode. Cook for about 30 minutes until the peppers are tender.
8. During the last 5 minutes of cooking, top each pepper with grated cheese and continue cooking until the cheese is melted and bubbly.
9. Garnish with fresh parsley leaves before serving.

Pork Schnitzel with Lemon-Dill Sauce

Prep Time: 15 minutes / Cook Time: 15 minutes
Servings: 4 / Mode: Air Fry

Ingredients:
- 4 pork loin cutlets
- 120g breadcrumbs

- 2 eggs, beaten
- 60ml vegetable oil
- 2 lemons, zested and juiced
- 2 tablespoons fresh dill, chopped
- Salt and black pepper, to taste

Preparation Instructions:

1. Preheat your dual zone air fryer to 375°F using the Air Fry mode.
2. Place the breadcrumbs on a plate and season with salt and black pepper.
3. Dip each pork cutlet into the beaten eggs, allowing any excess to drip off, and then coat it with breadcrumbs.
4. Place the breaded pork cutlets in the preheated air fryer using the Air Fry mode. Cook for about 10-15 minutes, turning halfway through, until the pork is golden brown and cooked through.
5. While the pork is cooking, prepare the lemon-dill sauce. In a bowl, combine lemon zest, lemon juice, and chopped dill. Season with salt and black pepper.
6. Serve the Pork Schnitzel hot, drizzled with the lemon-dill sauce.

Pork and Apricot Wellington

Prep Time: 30 minutes / Cook Time: 35 minutes
Servings: 4 / Mode: Bake

Ingredients:

- 4 pork loin medallions
- 2 sheets puff pastry
- 100g dried apricots, chopped
- 100g spinach leaves
- 1 egg, beaten (for egg wash)
- Salt and black pepper, to taste

Preparation Instructions:

1. Preheat your dual zone air fryer to 375°F using the Bake mode.
2. Season the pork loin medallions with salt and black pepper.
3. In a skillet, quickly sear the pork medallions over high heat for about 1-2 minutes on each side. Remove from heat and let them cool.
4. Roll out the puff pastry sheets and cut them into squares large enough to wrap around each pork medallion.
5. Place a layer of spinach leaves on each puff pastry square, followed by the seared pork medallion and

chopped apricots.
6. Brush the edges of the puff pastry with beaten egg, then fold the pastry over the pork and apricot filling, sealing the edges.
7. Place the pork Wellingtons in the preheated air fryer using the Bake mode. Cook for about 25-30 minutes or until the pastry is golden brown and the pork is cooked through.
8. Serve the Pork and Apricot Wellington hot with your favourite side dishes.

Pork and Sage-Stuffed Zucchini Boats

Prep Time: 20 minutes / Cook Time: 25 minutes
Servings: 4 / Mode: Bake

Ingredients:

- 4 large zucchini
- 500g ground pork
- 1 onion, chopped
- 2 cloves garlic, minced
- 12g fresh sage leaves, chopped
- 240ml tomato sauce
- 120g grated Parmesan cheese
- Salt and black pepper, to taste
- Olive oil (for drizzling)

Preparation Instructions:

1. Preheat your dual zone air fryer to 375°F using the Bake mode.
2. Cut the zucchini in half lengthwise and scoop out the seeds to create a hollow "boat."
3. In a skillet, heat some olive oil over medium heat. Add chopped onion and minced garlic, and sauté for about 2 minutes until softened.
4. Add the ground pork and cook until browned and cooked through. Stir in the chopped sage leaves and season with salt and black pepper.
5. Fill each zucchini boat with the pork and sage mixture.
6. Place the stuffed zucchini boats in the preheated air fryer using the Bake mode. Cook for about 25 minutes or until the zucchini is tender.
7. During the last 5 minutes of cooking, sprinkle grated Parmesan cheese over the zucchini boats and continue cooking until the cheese is melted and bubbly.
8. Serve the Pork and Sage-Stuffed Zucchini Boats hot, garnished with fresh sage leaves.

Beef and Black Bean Enchiladas

Prep Time: 25 minutes / Cook Time: 20 minutes
Servings: 4 / Mode: Bake

Ingredients:

- 500g ground beef
- 1 onion, chopped
- 2 cloves garlic, minced
- 400g black beans, drained and rinsed
- 240ml tomato sauce
- 1 teaspoon ground cumin
- 1 teaspoon chilli powder
- 8 small tortillas
- 200g shredded cheddar cheese
- Fresh cilantro leaves (for garnish)
- Sour cream (for serving)

Preparation Instructions:

1. Preheat your dual zone air fryer to 375°F using the Bake mode.
2. In a skillet, heat some olive oil over medium heat. Add chopped onion and minced garlic, and sauté for about 2 minutes until softened.
3. Add the ground beef and cook until browned. Drain any excess fat.
4. Stir in the black beans, tomato sauce, ground cumin, and Chilli powder. Simmer for about 5 minutes.
5. Place a spoonful of the beef and black bean mixture onto each tortilla, roll them up, and place them seam-side down in an ovenproof dish.
6. Sprinkle shredded cheddar cheese over the enchiladas.
7. Place the dish in the preheated air fryer using the Bake mode. Cook for about 15-20 minutes until the enchiladas are heated through, and the cheese is melted and bubbly.
8. Garnish with fresh cilantro leaves and serve the Beef and Black Bean Enchiladas hot with sour cream on the side.

Beef and Spinach Phyllo Triangles

Prep Time: 20 minutes / Cook Time: 20 minutes
Servings: 4 / Mode: Bake

Ingredients:

- 200g ground beef
- 1 small onion, finely chopped
- 2 cloves garlic, minced
- 200g fresh spinach, chopped
- 100g feta cheese, crumbled
- 2 tablespoons olive oil
- Salt and black pepper, to taste
- 8 sheets phyllo pastry
- Butter, melted (for brushing)
- Sesame seeds (for garnish)

Preparation Instructions:

1. Preheat your dual zone air fryer to 375°F using the Bake mode.
2. In a skillet, heat olive oil over medium heat. Add chopped onion and minced garlic, and sauté until softened, about 2 minutes.
3. Add the ground beef and cook until browned, breaking it up with a spoon as it cooks.
4. Stir in the chopped spinach and cook for another 2-3 minutes until wilted. Remove from heat and let it cool slightly.
5. Add crumbled feta cheese to the beef and spinach mixture. Season with salt and black pepper. Mix well.
6. Lay out one sheet of phyllo pastry and brush it lightly with melted butter. Place another sheet on top and repeat the process until you have a stack of 4 sheets.
7. Cut the stacked phyllo pastry into squares or rectangles, depending on your preference.
8. Place a spoonful of the beef and spinach mixture onto each square or rectangle. Fold the pastry over the filling to create triangles.
9. Brush the tops of the phyllo triangles with more melted butter and sprinkle with sesame seeds.
10. Place the triangles in the preheated air fryer using the Bake mode. Cook for about 15-20 minutes or until they are golden brown and crispy.
11. Serve the Beef and Spinach Phyllo Triangles hot!

Chapter 10 Dessert

Lemon and Thyme Shortbread

Prep Time: 15 minutes / Cook Time: 20 minutes
Servings: 16 pieces / Mode: Bake

Ingredients:

- 200g unsalted butter, softened
- 100g granulated sugar
- 300g all-purpose flour
- Zest of 2 lemons
- 5g fresh thyme leaves
- 2.5g salt
- Powdered sugar (for dusting)

Preparation Instructions:

1. Preheat your dual zone air fryer to 350°F using the Bake mode.
2. In a mixing bowl, cream together softened butter and granulated sugar until light and fluffy.
3. Add all-purpose flour, lemon zest, fresh thyme leaves, and salt to the butter mixture. Mix until a dough forms.
4. Roll out the dough on a floured surface to about 1/4-inch thickness.
5. Cut the dough into desired shapes using cookie cutters.
6. Place the shortbread cookies in the preheated air fryer using the Bake mode. Bake for about 12-15 minutes or until they are lightly golden.
7. Remove the Lemon and Thyme Shortbread from the air fryer and let them cool on a wire rack.
8. Dust with powdered sugar before serving.

Saffron and Cardamom Semolina Cake

Prep Time: 20 minutes / Cook Time: 30 minutes
Servings: 8 slices / Mode: Bake

Ingredients:

- 200g semolina
- 150g granulated sugar
- 200g plain yoghourt
- 60ml vegetable oil
- 5g saffron threads (soaked in 2 tablespoons of warm milk)
- 5g ground cardamom
- 10g baking powder
- 30g slivered almonds (for garnish)

Preparation Instructions:

1. Preheat your dual zone air fryer to 350°F using the Bake mode.
2. In a mixing bowl, combine semolina, granulated sugar, plain yogurt, vegetable oil, saffron (soaked in milk), ground cardamom, and baking powder. Mix until well combined.
3. Grease a cake pan and pour the semolina batter into it.
4. Sprinkle slivered almonds on top for garnish.
5. Place the cake pan in the preheated air fryer using the Bake mode. Bake for about 25-30 minutes or until the cake is firm and golden.
6. Remove the Saffron and Cardamom Semolina Cake from the air fryer and let it cool before slicing.

Lemon and Blueberry Cheesecake Bars

Prep Time: 20 minutes / Cook Time: 40 minutes
Servings: 12 bars / Mode: Bake

Ingredients:

- 200g graham cracker crumbs
- 100g unsalted butter, melted
- 400g cream cheese, softened
- 150g granulated sugar   • 2 large eggs
- Zest and juice of 2 lemons
- 150g fresh blueberries
- Powdered sugar (for dusting)

Preparation Instructions:

1. Preheat your dual zone air fryer to 350°F using the Bake mode.
2. In a bowl, combine graham cracker crumbs and melted butter. Press the mixture into the bottom of a greased square baking pan to form the crust.
3. In a separate bowl, beat softened cream cheese and granulated sugar until smooth and creamy.
4. Add eggs, lemon zest, and lemon juice to the cream cheese mixture. Mix until well combined.
5. Pour the cream cheese mixture over the graham cracker crust.
6. Sprinkle fresh blueberries evenly over the cheesecake layer.
7. Place the baking pan in the preheated air fryer using the Bake mode. Bake for about 35-40 minutes or until the cheesecake is set and edges are lightly golden.
8. Remove the Lemon and Blueberry Cheesecake Bars from the air fryer and let them cool.
9. Once cooled, refrigerate the bars for a few hours or until they are chilled.
10. Dust with powdered sugar before serving.

Rosewater and Pistachio Mille-Feuille

Prep Time: 20 minutes / Cook Time: 20 minutes
Servings: 4 / Mode: Bake

Ingredients:

- 1 sheet of puff pastry
- 100g pistachios, chopped
- 150ml heavy cream
- 30g powdered sugar
- 5ml rosewater
- Edible rose petals (for garnish)

Preparation Instructions:

1. Preheat your dual zone air fryer to 375°F using the Bake mode.
2. Cut the puff pastry sheet into 8 equal-sized rectangles.
3. Place the pastry rectangles in the preheated air fryer using the Bake mode. Bake for about 8-10 minutes until they puff up and are golden brown.
4. While the pastry is baking, whip the heavy cream with powdered sugar and rosewater until stiff peaks form.
5. Once the pastry rectangles are done, let them cool.
6. To assemble, place a puff pastry rectangle on a plate, spread a layer of whipped cream, sprinkle chopped pistachios, and repeat the layers.
7. Finish with a puff pastry rectangle on top and a dusting of powdered sugar.
8. Garnish with edible rose petals.

Blackberry and Almond Frangipane Tartlets

Prep Time: 20 minutes / Cook Time: 25 minutes
Servings: 6 tartlets / Mode: Bake

Ingredients:

- 1 sheet of store-bought puff pastry
- 100g almond paste
- 50g unsalted butter, softened
- 1 egg
- 100g fresh blackberries
- Sliced almonds (for garnish)
- Powdered sugar (for dusting)

Preparation Instructions:

1. Preheat your dual zone air fryer to 375°F using the Bake mode.
2. Cut the puff pastry sheet into 6 circles to fit your tartlet molds.
3. In a bowl, mix almond paste, softened butter, and egg until smooth.
4. Spread the almond mixture evenly over the puff pastry circles.
5. Arrange fresh blackberries on top of the almond mixture.
6. Place the tartlets in the preheated air fryer using the Bake mode. Bake for about 20-25 minutes until the pastry is golden brown and the frangipane is set.
7. Remove the Blackberry and Almond Frangipane Tartlets from the air fryer.
8. Garnish with sliced almonds and a dusting of powdered sugar.

Chocolate Hazelnut Stuffed Dates

Prep Time:b15 minutes / Cook Time: 3 minutes
Servings: 12 stuffed dates / Mode: Max Crisp

Ingredients:

- 12 Medjool dates, pitted
- 12 whole roasted hazelnuts
- 50g dark chocolate, melted

Preparation Instructions:

1. Preheat your dual zone air fryer to the Max Crisp mode.
2. Slice each Medjool date lengthwise to create an opening.
3. Stuff each date with a whole roasted hazelnut.
4. Drizzle melted dark chocolate over the stuffed dates.
5. Place the stuffed dates in the preheated air fryer using the Max Crisp mode for about 2-3 minutes, just until the chocolate sets.
6. Remove the Chocolate Hazelnut Stuffed Dates from the air fryer and let them cool before serving.

Lemon and Poppy Seed Biscuits

Prep Time: 15 minutes / Cook Time: 12 minutes
Servings: 24 biscuits / Mode: Bake

Ingredients:

- 200g unsalted butter, softened
- 150g granulated sugar
- Zest of 2 lemons
- 1 large egg
- 300g all-purpose flour
- 10g poppy seeds

Preparation Instructions:

1. Preheat your dual zone air fryer to 350°F using the Bake mode.
2. In a mixing bowl, cream together softened butter, granulated sugar, and lemon zest until light and fluffy.
3. Add the egg and mix until well combined.
4. Gradually add all-purpose flour and poppy seeds to

form a cookie dough.

5. Roll the dough into small balls and place them on a baking sheet.

6. Flatten each ball with a fork to create a crisscross pattern.

7. Place the biscuits in the preheated air fryer using the Bake mode. Bake for about 10-12 minutes or until they are lightly golden.

8. Remove the Lemon and Poppy Seed Biscuits from the air fryer and let them cool on a wire rack.

Earl Grey Tea Infused Creme Brulee

Prep Time: 20 minutes / Cook Time: 45 minutes
Servings: 4 / Mode: Bake

Ingredients:

- 240ml heavy cream
- 2 Earl Grey tea bags
- 4 egg yolks
- 80g granulated sugar
- 5ml vanilla extract
- Extra granulated sugar (for caramelising)

Preparation Instructions:

1. Preheat your dual zone air fryer to 325°F using the Bake mode.

2. In a saucepan, heat heavy cream until it begins to simmer. Remove from heat, add Earl Grey tea bags, and steep for 10 minutes. Remove tea bags and discard.

3. In a separate bowl, whisk together egg yolks and granulated sugar until well combined.

4. Slowly pour the infused cream into the egg yolk mixture, whisking continuously.

5. Stir in vanilla extract.

6. Pour the mixture into four ramekins.

7. Place the ramekins in the preheated air fryer using the Bake mode. Bake for about 35-45 minutes or until the custard is set around the edges but still slightly jiggly in the centre.

8. Remove the Earl Grey Tea Infused Creme Brulee from the air fryer and let them cool to room temperature. Then refrigerate for a few hours until chilled.

9. Just before serving, sprinkle a thin layer of granulated sugar on top of each custard and caramelise.

Raspberry and Pistachio Baked Alaska

Prep Time: 25 minutes / Cook Time: 5 minutes
Servings: 4 / Mode: Bake

Ingredients:

- 4 slices of sponge cake
- 200g raspberry sorbet
- 4 large scoops of pistachio ice cream
- 4 egg whites
- 150g granulated sugar

Preparation Instructions:

1. Preheat your dual zone air fryer to 400°F using the Bake mode.

2. Place a slice of sponge cake on a baking sheet.

3. Top each sponge cake slice with a scoop of raspberry sorbet and a scoop of pistachio ice cream. Press the ice cream down gently.

4. In a bowl, beat the egg whites until stiff peaks form. Gradually add granulated sugar while continuing to beat until you have a glossy meringue.

5. Spread the meringue over the ice cream and sponge cake, making sure to seal the edges.

6. Place the baking sheet in the preheated air fryer using the Bake mode for about 3-5 minutes or until the meringue is lightly browned.

7. Remove the Raspberry and Pistachio Baked Alaska from the air fryer and serve immediately.

Cardamom and Orange Blossom Eclairs

Prep Time: 30 minutes / Cook Time: 20 minutes
Servings: 12 eclairs / Mode: Bake

Ingredients:

- For the choux pastry:
- 125g all-purpose flour
- 100ml water
- 100ml milk
- 80g unsalted butter
- 3 large eggs
- 5g ground cardamom
- For the filling:
- 300ml heavy cream
- 30g powdered sugar
- 5ml orange blossom water
- For the glaze:
- 100g dark chocolate, melted

Preparation Instructions:

- For the choux pastry:

1. Preheat your dual zone air fryer to 375°F using the Bake mode.

2. In a saucepan, combine water, milk, butter, and ground cardamom. Bring to a boil.

3. Remove from heat and quickly stir in all-purpose flour until a smooth dough forms.

4. Let the dough cool slightly, then add eggs one at a time, mixing well after each addition until the dough is glossy.
5. Transfer the choux pastry dough to a piping bag and pipe 12 eclairs onto a baking sheet.
6. Place the baking sheet in the preheated air fryer using the Bake mode. Bake for about 15-20 minutes or until the eclairs are golden brown and puffed.

For the filling:
7. In a bowl, whip heavy cream, powdered sugar, and orange blossom water until stiff peaks form.
8. Once the eclairs are cooled, slice them in half horizontally and fill with the whipped cream mixture.

For the glaze:
9. Drizzle melted dark chocolate over the filled eclairs.
10. Let the chocolate set before serving your Cardamom and Orange Blossom Eclairs.

Lemon Lavender Madeleines

Prep Time: 20 minutes / Cook Time: 10 minutes
Servings: 12 madeleines / Mode: Bake

Ingredients:
- 2 large eggs
- 100g granulated sugar
- 125g all-purpose flour
- 5g dried lavender flowers
- Zest of 1 lemon
- 10ml lemon juice
- 100g unsalted butter, melted and cooled

Preparation Instructions:
1. Preheat your dual zone air fryer to 350°F using the Bake mode.
2. In a bowl, whisk together eggs and granulated sugar until light and fluffy.
3. Gradually fold in all-purpose flour, dried lavender flowers, lemon zest, lemon juice, and melted butter until you have a smooth batter.
4. Grease madeleine molds and spoon the batter into each mold, filling them about 2/3 full.
5. Place the madeleine molds in the preheated air fryer using the Bake mode. Bake for about 8-10 minutes or until the madeleines are golden brown and have a slight hump.
6. Remove the Lemon Lavender Madeleines from the air fryer and let them cool before serving.

Cinnamon Sugar Churros with Chocolate Dipping Sauce

Prep Time: 20 minutes / Cook Time: 15 minutes
Servings: 4 / Mode: Max Crisp

Ingredients:
- For the churros:
- 200g all-purpose flour
- 240ml water
- 30g granulated sugar
- 30g unsalted butter
- 5g salt
- 2 large eggs
- 10ml vanilla extract
- Vegetable oil (for frying)
- For the cinnamon sugar coating:
- 100g granulated sugar
- 10g ground cinnamon
- For the chocolate dipping sauce:
- 100g dark chocolate, chopped
- 120ml heavy cream

Preparation Instructions:
For the churros:
1. Preheat your dual zone air fryer to the Max Crisp mode.
2. In a saucepan, combine water, granulated sugar, unsalted butter, and salt. Bring to a boil.
3. Remove from heat and quickly stir in all-purpose flour until a smooth dough forms.
4. Let the dough cool slightly, then add eggs one at a time, mixing well after each addition until the dough is glossy.
5. Transfer the churro dough to a piping bag fitted with a star tip.
6. Heat vegetable oil in a deep skillet or pan. Pipe strips of churro dough directly into the hot oil and fry until golden brown, about 2-3 minutes per side. Drain on paper towels.

For the cinnamon sugar coating:
7. In a bowl, mix granulated sugar and ground cinnamon.
8. While the churros are still warm, roll them in the cinnamon sugar mixture until coated.

For the chocolate dipping sauce:
9. In a microwave-safe bowl, heat heavy cream until hot but not boiling. Add chopped dark chocolate and stir until smooth.
10. Serve the Cinnamon Sugar Churros with the warm chocolate dipping sauce.

Rosewater and Pistachio Baklava

Prep Time: 30 minutes / Cook Time: 45 minutes
Servings: 24 baklava pieces / Mode: Bake

Ingredients:
- 1 package (16 ounces) phyllo pastry sheets, thawed

- 250g unsalted butter, melted
- 300g pistachios, finely chopped
- 150g granulated sugar
- 10ml rosewater
- 240ml honey
- Zest of 1 lemon
- Juice of 1 lemon

Preparation Instructions:

1. Preheat your dual zone air fryer to 350°F using the Bake mode.
2. In a bowl, combine chopped pistachios, granulated sugar, rosewater, lemon zest, and lemon juice. Mix well to make the filling.
3. Brush a baking dish with melted butter.
4. Place one phyllo sheet in the dish and brush it with more melted butter. Repeat this process, layering and buttering each sheet, until you have about 8 layers.
5. Spread a layer of the pistachio filling over the phyllo layers.
6. Continue layering phyllo sheets, butter, and pistachio filling until all filling is used, finishing with a final layer of phyllo sheets.
7. Cut the baklava into diamond or square shapes.
8. Bake in the preheated air fryer using the Bake mode for about 40-45 minutes or until the baklava is golden brown and crisp.
9. While the baklava is baking, heat honey in a saucepan until it becomes thin and runny.
10. Once the baklava is done, remove it from the air fryer and immediately pour the hot honey evenly over it.
11. Let the Rosewater and Pistachio Baklava cool completely before serving.

Orange and Almond Polenta Cake

Prep Time: 15 minutes / Cook Time: 40 minutes
Servings: 8 / Mode: Bake

Ingredients:

- 150g unsalted butter, softened
- 150g granulated sugar
- 3 large eggs
- Zest and juice of 2 oranges
- 150g almond meal
- 100g fine polenta
- 5g baking powder
- Powdered sugar (for dusting)

Preparation Instructions:

1. Preheat your dual zone air fryer to 350°F using the Bake mode.
2. In a mixing bowl, cream together softened butter and granulated sugar until light and fluffy.
3. Add eggs one at a time, beating well after each addition.
4. Stir in the zest and juice of 2 oranges.
5. In a separate bowl, combine almond meal, fine polenta, and baking powder.
6. Gradually add the dry ingredients to the wet ingredients and mix until well combined.
7. Pour the batter into a greased cake pan.
8. Place the cake pan in the preheated air fryer using the Bake mode for about 35-40 minutes or until a toothpick inserted into the centre comes out clean.
9. Remove the Orange and Almond Polenta Cake from the air fryer and let it cool.
10. Dust with powdered sugar before serving.

Coffee and Walnut Swiss Roll

Prep Time: 20 minutes / Cook Time: 12 minutes
Servings: 8 / Mode: Bake

Ingredients:

- For the sponge:
- 3 large eggs
- 75g granulated sugar
- 75g self-raising flour
- 10g instant coffee granules, dissolved in 10ml hot water
- 30g chopped walnuts
- For the filling:
- 150ml double cream
- 30g icing sugar
- 10g instant coffee granules, dissolved in 10ml hot water

Preparation Instructions:

1. Preheat your dual zone air fryer to 350°F using the Bake mode.
2. In a mixing bowl, beat eggs and granulated sugar together until light and fluffy.
3. Gently fold in the self-raising flour until well combined.
4. Add the dissolved coffee and chopped walnuts to the batter, folding until evenly mixed.
5. Pour the batter into a greased and lined Swiss roll tin.
6. Bake in the preheated air fryer using the Bake mode for about 10-12 minutes or until the sponge is lightly golden and springs back when touched.
7. While the sponge is baking, prepare the filling. Whip the double cream and icing sugar until it forms soft peaks. Gently fold in the dissolved coffee.
8. Once the sponge is done, remove it from the air fryer, and immediately turn it out onto a clean tea towel dusted with icing sugar.
9. Carefully roll up the sponge with the tea towel and

leave it to cool.

10. Unroll the sponge, spread the coffee cream filling evenly, and roll it back up.

11. Slice and serve your delicious Coffee and Walnut Swiss Roll.

Ginger and Orange Biscotti

Prep Time: 15 minutes / Baking Time: 35 minutes
Servings: About 20 biscotti / Mode: Bake

Ingredients:

- 200g all-purpose flour
- 150g granulated sugar
- 2 large eggs
- Zest of 1 orange
- 1 teaspoon ground ginger
- 1/2 teaspoon baking powder
- A pinch of salt

Preparation Instructions:

1. Preheat your dual zone air fryer to 325°F using the Bake mode.

2. In a mixing bowl, combine all-purpose flour, granulated sugar, ground ginger, baking powder, and a pinch of salt.

3. In a separate bowl, whisk the eggs and orange zest together.

4. Gradually add the egg mixture to the dry ingredients, mixing until a stiff dough forms.

5. Divide the dough in half and shape each half into a log on a parchment-lined baking sheet.

6. Bake in the preheated air fryer using the Bake mode for about 30-35 minutes or until the logs are lightly golden and firm to the touch.

7. Remove the biscotti logs from the air fryer and let them cool for a few minutes.

8. Slice the logs into biscotti-sized pieces and place them back on the baking sheet.

9. Return the biscotti to the air fryer using the Bake mode and bake for an additional 10-15 minutes, flipping them halfway through, until they are crispy and golden.

10. Let the Ginger and Orange Biscotti cool completely before enjoying.

Pecan and Maple Syrup Bread Pudding

Prep Time: 15 minutes / Baking Time: 35 minutes
Servings: 6 / Mode: Bake

Ingredients:

- 4 slices of stale bread, cubed
- 100g pecans, chopped
- 2 large eggs
- 240ml milk
- 80ml maple syrup
- 5g ground cinnamon
- 5g vanilla extract
- A pinch of salt

Preparation Instructions:

1. Preheat your dual zone air fryer to 350°F using the Bake mode.

2. In a mixing bowl, whisk together eggs, milk, maple syrup, ground cinnamon, vanilla extract, and a pinch of salt.

3. Add the cubed stale bread and chopped pecans to the egg mixture. Stir until all the bread is soaked.

4. Grease a baking dish and transfer the bread pudding mixture into it.

5. Bake in the preheated air fryer using the Bake mode for about 30-35 minutes or until the pudding is set and the top is golden brown.

6. Remove the Pecan and Maple Syrup Bread Pudding from the air fryer, let it cool slightly, and serve warm.

Coconut and Lime Madeleines

Prep Time: 15 minutes / Baking Time: 10 minutes
Servings: About 12 madeleines / Mode: Bake

Ingredients:

- 2 large eggs
- 100g granulated sugar
- 120g all-purpose flour
- 1 teaspoon baking powder
- 60g unsalted butter, melted
- Zest of 1 lime
- 30g desiccated coconut

Preparation Instructions:

1. Preheat your dual zone air fryer to 350°F using the Bake mode.

2. In a mixing bowl, whisk together eggs and granulated sugar until pale and fluffy.

3. Sift all-purpose flour and baking powder into the egg mixture, and gently fold until just combined.

4. Stir in melted butter, lime zest, and desiccated coconut.

5. Grease and flour madeleine molds.

6. Spoon the batter into each madeleine mold, filling them about 2/3 full.

7. Bake in the preheated air fryer using the Bake mode for about 8-10 minutes or until the madeleines are golden brown and spring back when touched.

8. Remove the Coconut and Lime Madeleines from the air fryer, let them cool slightly, and enjoy.

Banana Fritters with Butterscotch Sauce

Prep Time: 15 minutes / Cook Time: 10 minutes
Servings: About 4 servings / Mode: Air Fry

Ingredients:

- 2 ripe bananas, peeled and sliced
- 100g all-purpose flour
- 5g baking powder
- A pinch of salt
- 30g granulated sugar
- 120ml milk
- Vegetable oil (for frying)
- Powdered sugar (for dusting)
- For the Butterscotch Sauce:
- 60g unsalted butter
- 60g brown sugar
- 60ml heavy cream

Preparation Instructions:

1. Preheat your dual zone air fryer to 375°F using the Air Fry mode.
2. In a mixing bowl, combine all-purpose flour, baking powder, salt, and granulated sugar.
3. Gradually add milk and whisk until a smooth batter forms.
4. Dip banana slices into the batter, coating them evenly.
5. Place the battered banana slices in the air fryer basket, leaving space between each slice.
6. Air fry for about 5-6 minutes or until the banana fritters are golden and crispy.
7. While the banana fritters are cooking, make the butterscotch sauce. In a saucepan, melt butter over medium heat. Stir in brown sugar until it's dissolved. Add heavy cream and stir until the sauce thickens.
8. Remove the banana fritters from the air fryer, let them cool slightly, and dust with powdered sugar. Drizzle with butterscotch sauce and serve.

Spiced Carrot and Walnut Cake

Prep Time: 20 minutes / Baking Time: 35-40 minutes
Servings: 12 slices / Mode: Bake

Ingredients:

- 200g all-purpose flour
- 200g granulated sugar
- 200ml vegetable oil
- 3 large eggs
- 200g carrots, grated
- 100g walnuts, chopped
- 1 teaspoon ground cinnamon
- 1/2 teaspoon ground nutmeg
- 1/2 teaspoon ground ginger
- 1 teaspoon baking powder
- 1/2 teaspoon baking soda
- A pinch of salt
- Zest of 1 orange
- Zest of 1 lemon
- For the Cream Cheese Frosting:
- 200g cream cheese, softened
- 100g unsalted butter, softened
- 200g powdered sugar
- 1 teaspoon vanilla extract
- Zest of 1 orange (optional)

Preparation Instructions:

1. Preheat your dual zone air fryer to 350°F using the Bake mode.
2. In a mixing bowl, whisk together all-purpose flour, granulated sugar, ground cinnamon, ground nutmeg, ground ginger, baking powder, baking soda, and a pinch of salt.
3. In another bowl, beat the eggs and add vegetable oil, grated carrots, chopped walnuts, and the zest of 1 orange and 1 lemon. Mix well.
4. Gradually add the wet mixture to the dry ingredients and stir until just combined.
5. Grease and flour a round cake pan.
6. Pour the cake batter into the prepared pan.
7. Bake in the preheated air fryer using the Bake mode for about 35-40 minutes or until a toothpick inserted into the centre comes out clean.
8. While the cake is baking, prepare the cream cheese frosting. In a separate bowl, beat together cream cheese and softened butter until creamy and smooth. Gradually add powdered sugar and vanilla extract. Mix until well combined. Stir in the zest of 1 orange if desired.
9. Once the cake is done, remove it from the air fryer and let it cool in the pan for a few minutes.
10. Transfer the cake to a wire rack to cool completely.
11. Once the cake has cooled, spread the cream cheese frosting on top.
12. Slice and serve your delicious Spiced Carrot and Walnut Cake.

Printed in Great Britain
by Amazon

31626655R00044